The Spiritual Gas Up

365 Quotes and Affirmations for Daily Motivation

By Jai Marie Harris

The Spiritual Gas Up

ISBN-13: 978-1-7366962-7-9

Dedication

This book is dedicated to Alexis J Fields. Thank you for being my inspiration and my guide in life and in death. You have motivated me to always be the best version of myself and to make the most of this lifetime ever since yours was cut short. For that I am forever grateful…

Jai

The Spiritual Gas Up

Introduction

W e are so used to the custom of looking at the start of a new year as a beginning point to stay charged up and motivated. As a way to make things happen in life. This tends to create a high of motivation that usually withers after three months into the year. But the year is still going and you are still breathing. After those first three month most of us need a boost or better yet, to add a little gas in our physical, mental and spiritual tank. Whether you are starting in January, July, or December, "The Spiritual Gas Up" gives you an opportunity to gas yourself up and stay ready in order to handle those blockages in this road called life.

"The Spiritual Gas Up" is a tool that does this by providing you with quotes, affirmations, and various activities. It's a boost and a motivator that will lead to inspiration and fire up the goals you have in that beautiful mind of yours. Working on you is a lifetime journey which does not have to start New Year's Day. Delve into this piece of inspiration to stay motivated all year long.

Day 1

"Bosses do what they want, and others do what they can."

W hich one will you choose to be today? Don't allow fear to put you outside of your greatness while allowing you to settle for the minimum. Know and believe that you have everything it takes to be great today. Being a boss is not just a title, it's a state of mind.

Today's Affirmation:
I AM A BOSS, BECAUSE I SAID SO!

Day 2

"My energy exudes royalty with or without the crown."

I f you don't know and assert your value, it's going to be pretty hard for anyone else to. Life will always serve its ups and downs. We are always going to be presented with decisions and respond to them in ways that we aren't proud of. Don't shame yourself. Understand that our past mishaps don't define us, and it definitely does not take away from our worth. You are perfectly imperfect and there is only one you. Remember that, know that.

Today's Affirmation:
I AM THE QUEEN/ I AM THE KING!

Day 3

"You are invaluable, so it is not enough to just add tax. Know your worth and add tax, processing fees, service charge, and a time investment share."

Sometimes people keep us around simply because we are an asset to them. In life it is an act of love and service to give. However, understand when people are trying to deplete you and run you dry. Time is like money; it should never be wasted. Know your value first whether others see it or not.

Today's Affirmation:
I AM ALWAYS WORTHY!

Day 4

"I stopped waiting for the light at the end of the tunnel and I lit that ish up myself."

There have been a lot of situations where I have heard people, myself included, say things like: When I lose this weight, I am going to do this or when I get this amount of money, I am going to do that. I learned that those phrases definitely put a pause on living in the present. It is imperative that we live for today while we still have breath in our body. We do not know what tomorrow holds. You don't want to go into tomorrow wishing you would have lived for today.

Today's Affirmation:
I DESERVE ALL THE GOOD THINGS IN LIFE!

Day 5

"Trusting your intuition is believing everything you feel, half of what you see, none of what you hear."

Often times we get a feeling about something and we talk ourselves out of it and we regret not taking heed to the initial feeling. When we feel things in our body, we can usually sense whether it's a good thing or a bad thing. We get sensations that feel like they are specifically communicating through our hearts or guts telling us that something just isn't right. This is what is known as our intuition, it's our bodies warning that something may not be what it appears to be. It is important to pay attention to the thoughts and feelings that occur in your body. These feelings will save you from anything that isn't for you.

Today's Affirmation:
I AM DESERVING OF RECIPROCITY!

Day 6

"Sacrifices create the formula for success."

Very seldom in life do you find reward without risk. Whether it's with work/business, love or growth development in general. If we want our circumstances to change, most of the time, we have to do something we have never done before. Take that leap of faith. Step out of your comfort zone today, it may change your circumstances for the better. What do you have to lose?

Today's Affirmation:
I AM SUCCESSFUL BY MY STANDARDS!

Day 7

*"Don't let life pass you by because your allowing
energy vampires to suck you dry."*

Emotional reciprocity is what happens in a relationship when there are equal parts of give and take. It's a mutually beneficial relationship where there is balance. This is key. Don't let these moochers tip the scale

Today's Affirmation:

I ONLY ATTRACT THOSE WITH GOOD
INTENTIONS IN MY LIFE!

Day 8

"Don't count on court jesters to help you make royal decisions."

Not everyone around is on your journey to assist in accomplishing your goals within your life path. Some people who appear to be helpful may actually be distractions. Pay attention to the energy the people around you exude. If your goal is to obtain positivity but your "friend" is always negative or you're trying to obtain financial freedom, but your girlfriend seems to encourage you to participate in frivolous spending. Make sure the circle you keep is filled with individuals who are on the same path and not those who are simply there as speed bumps.

Today's Affirmation:
I AM APART OF A WINNING TEAM!

Day 9

"My self-love has become my best love; the love of my life."

How can you properly allow anyone to love on you if you are unaware of how to love on yourself? One of the most important life lessons is to know and practice loving yourself always. The only relationship that is guaranteed for a lifetime is the one you have with yourself.

Today's Affirmation:

I AM LOVED; THEREFORE, I RECEIVE AND GIVE LOVE!

Day 10

"Turning your losses into lessons will always be a blessing."

Watching something not happen the way you expected to can be an emotionally trying situation. No one goes into anything saying I hope this fails or it would be great if this didn't turn out right. So, when it happens it can bring up feelings of shame, guilt and failure. Don't fret, everything happens for a reason. It's hard to see it when you're in it but eventually we come to a realization and we end up learning from it if we choose to. This teaches us how to not give up and how to move differently. There are no failures just moments of being knocked off track.

Today's Affirmation:

I AM ALWAYS TAKEN CARE OF NO MATTER THE CIRCUMSTANCE!

Day 11

"Always choose yourself first and when in doubt choose yourself again."

Too often in life we end up placing ourselves last on the priority list. This sometimes puts us in a place of neglecting our own happiness and priorities. Today intentionally do something for you. Something that doesn't involve anyone else. This something can range from going to buy yourself something nice or just simply cancelling plans to just rest and be. You never have to feel guilty for choosing you first. The relationship you have with yourself is the most important relationship you will have. So, love you like you would want someone to.

Today's Affirmation:
I AM MORE THAN ENOUGH JUST THE WAY I AM!

Day 12

"Put in the work today because the time is going to pass anyway."

What are you waiting for? Don't say the right time or the right amount of money or this exact weight. Even if those things are a factor there is something you can do to start. So, what are you really waiting for? Planning is a way to start, utilizing mentorship by taking notes from someone already doing it is a start. Studying and researching is another way to start. Just start. It doesn't have to be perfect you just have to put one foot in front of the other.

Today's Affirmation:
SUCCESS AND MONEY FLOW TO ME
NATURALLY!

Day 13

"What's understood to those backstage does not always need to be explained to the audience."

In life a lot of the time we seek approval from others before we consult with ourselves or we allow the opinions of others to dictate the decisions we make. Make sure those you seek approval from are those who have experienced the paths you are attempting to embark on. Make sure they aren't projecting their fears on to your dreams. When you want to finalize a vision or dream give yourself the final say so in the decision.

Today's Affirmation:
I AM STRONG AND POWERFUL!

Day 14

"Only go and only stay where you are respected, loved and accepted."

L ife is too short to spend time in places where you are not valued. Time is something that has no currency because it is invaluable. Don't allow people and places that don't serve you to waste it.

Today's Affirmation:
I AM WORTHY OF RESPECT!

Day 15

*"Disconnected relationships aren't beef; it just means
you aren't vibrating on the same frequency anymore."*

Some relationships, friendships and associations come with a time stamp. If your involved in something that is taking more from you than you are receiving that may mean it has expired and it's time to let it go. This doesn't have to happen with anger it just needs to be understood that people grow apart and that is okay. Trust the process and appreciate the experience and the lessons as a whole.

Today's Affirmation:
I WALK AWAY FROM THINGS THAT
NO LONGER SERVE ME!

Day 16

"Your thoughts create your reality, make sure what you're telling yourself is loving and positive."

The things that occur in our minds are significantly powerful. So much so that you end up believing it. If you tell yourself you can't do something, or you won't have something it will become your reality. In this instance if you don't believe, it's best to fake it 'til you make it. The more you tell yourself: I can start that business, I can have that home, I will finish that class with an A, the more you will begin to see things lining up to help you obtain those desires. But it all starts in the mind. Change your mind, change your reality.

Today's Affirmation:
I AM DESERVING OF ALL THE GOOD THAT IS COMING INTO MY LIFE!

Day 17

"What negative people feel and think about me is none of my business."

Wh" hen people are critical of you for no apparent reason it usually has more to do with how they feel about themselves and less about how they feel about you. Everything is based on each individual's perception. If they want to waste their time letting you roam free in their mind, let them and continue to give them something to think about.

Today's Affirmation:
HATERS HAVE NO AFFECT OVER MY LIFE!

Day 18

"On life's journey don't let the bumps in the road make you fold. Stand firm on ten toes and fight to meet your goals."

Life will have its interruptions and they won't be easy, and some will even change you. It's important to feel in those hard times but don't let it consume you. Give yourself space to work through it. They won't last forever and there will be better days ahead. Its ok to recognize the negative while hoping for the positive. You will get through this, you always do.

Today's Affirmation:
I WILL MEET ALL MY GOALS!

Day 19

"Happiness and inner peace are a choice, even in the midst of utter chaos both feelings are able to reside within."

Being unbothered when there is madness occurring in your environment is definitely a skill. It doesn't always come naturally and often it has to be developed. Whenever you're in a space of not feeling happy or peaceful, a way to build that up is by writing three things you're grateful for. This could be something as small as I am thankful for air, I am thankful for my legs, I am thankful for the ability to see, etc. This will lead to creating thoughts of happiness in your brain. Try it.

Today's Affirmation:
TODAY AND EVERYDAY I CHOOSE HAPPINESS!

Day 20

"Life is about growing and glowing and if the people around aren't pouring into you, it's time to cut them loose."

Y ou really can go as far as the people in your circle are going. Look around at the company you keep. Are these people making strides in life? Are they individuals you can learn from? Do a quick check in with yourself and determine if the people around you are helping you grow to be a better version of you.

Today's Affirmation:

I AM ALWAYS GROWING INTO THE BETTER VERSION OF MYSELF!

Day 21

"You have the right to change your mind at any time."

This statement is true whether people agree with you or not. If something does not resonate with who you are as a person or if you no longer feel comfortable you can choose to walk away in the beginning, middle and even the end of it. This goes with any time and any situation. Good or bad.

Today's Affirmation:
I AM IN CONTROL OF MY LIFE!

Day 22

*"Keep in mind the same lessons will show up over and
over until you consciously show that you have learned
from them."*

The definition of insanity is repeating the
same thing over and over again and
expecting different results. When things
fail or don't work out, take what worked, leave
what didn't and try something different. Don't
be insane, that is like tripping over the same
crack in the road everyday instead of walking
around it. Once a lesson is complete don't pick
it up again. Leave it, take the pieces that worked
and move right along.

Today's Affirmation:
*I WILL ALWAYS BE BLESSED AFTER
MY LESSONS!*

Day 23

Fill up your tank.

Grand rising! Get your day started and write down one thing that you're grateful for, one thing that you love, one thing that makes you sad, and one thing that makes you happy. All of these emotions are a part of you, feel them and express them in healthy ways.

Today's Affirmation:

I HAVE A LOT TO BE GRATEFUL FOR AND THE BLESSINGS CONTINUE TO FLOW!

Day 24

"Know who you are at all times so those who don't know themselves don't come try to convince you otherwise."

It's important that you stand firm in your convictions and beliefs even if others don't. Everyone is not going to agree with you or even like you but that doesn't necessarily mean you have to conform to their criticism. If you love you that is really all that matters in the beginning and the end.

Today's Affirmation:
I AM THE BEST VERSION OF MYSELF!

Day 25

Fill your tank:

G et your day started by writing down five things you're proud of. If you can't think of five things ask someone who knows you what you have done to make them proud, fill in the blanks you left open with their answers.

Today's Affirmation:

*I AM ALWAYS PROUD OF THE PERSON
I AM!*

Day 26

"Don't allow the opinions of others to dictate the way you move. Trust yourself always."

Along your journey, whether it is the road to self-discovery, or just success in general, you will find people who are here for you and others who are trying to deter you. Stay the course and be open to learning from everybody and create an awareness to recognize those who are trying to get through you.

Today's Affirmation:
I AM ON THE PERFECT PATH FOR ME!

Day 27

"Do everything with good intentions and the outcome will work in your favor."

Karma is very real and is the balancing act of the universe. The better you put out the more you receive. Make sure you create an awareness for those who truly appreciate the love you give and the good energy you provide but be weary of those who may take advantage of it.

Today's Affirmation:

I DO EVERYTHING WITH GOOD INTENTIONS WHICH IS WHY BLESSINGS FLOW TO ME!

Day 28

Live your life in truth and honesty.

If this is what you want to receive it is important you put it out. This starts by you giving it to yourself first. Sometimes the truth hurts as the immediate outcome, but a lie can have harsher consequences once discovered later.

Today's Affirmation:

I AM THE TRUTH; THEREFORE, I ONLY ATTRACT HONESTY IN MY LIFE!

Day 29

"Personal unhappiness for another person's behavior is your inability to accept them for who they are."

People can only be as elevated as the amount of healing they have put into themselves. Whatever they have poured into themselves or lack thereof will only overflow into the areas of their lives. Are you allowing the cups of negative people to constantly poor out on to you? How does it feel? When will you move out of the way?

Today's Affirmation:
I SURROUND MYSELF WITH PEOPLE WHO LOVE ON ME!

Day 30

"True love is free from obsession and control."

When you truly love someone, you appreciate them for who they are as a person. Although some of the characteristics may not be totally in alignment with what you're used to, but you appreciate them anyway. When you love someone there should never be a tussle for control to get them to accept you or love you back. That is just an ongoing tug of war where no one comes out a winner.

Today's Affirmation:
I AM BLESSED WITH LOVE AND
LIGHT!

Day 31

"Stay in your lane where the road is paved and there is no traffic."

I f we are constantly looking back or to the side while going forward its showing that we are more focused on everyone else winning. Well what about you? Don't you deserve to win? Focus on your path in the present to get where you need to go, and you can help others once you get there.

Today's Affirmation:

I AM THE DRIVER OF MY LIFE AND MY ROAD IS FREE AND CLEAR!

Day 32

"Don't argue with fools, it may make it difficult for the audience to distinguish who is who."

Some people are determined to never understand you and that is okay. Why do you need to convince people where you are coming from when half the time they don't even know where they are going? Most people have made up perceptions of us in their head. They have made up their mind. Don't waste your time trying to change it. You will start to look just as crazy as they do.

Today's Affirmation:
I AM CLEAR OF ALL NEGATIVITY!

Day 33

"Disagreements happen, debates win trophies, but arguments are time wasted with no reward."

There are obvious differences between a disagreement, debate and an argument. Most arguments involve nonproductive conversations that lead to even more misunderstandings. Don't listen to argue, listen to understand. Have conversations that are productive if this is a person worth that time. If not, let it be. If you let it go what is the worst that can happen?

Today's Affirmation:
I ONLY ATTRACT POSITIVE ENERGY INTO MY LIFE!

Day 34

"Too blessed to be stressed and too quick on my toes to let anyone finesse."

It is important to maneuver through this life with love and light however that may not be a daily situation. There will be some days where people will test you. You let them know that they are going to end up failing. Just because you are the light does not mean you don't have that fire in you to protect yourself from the toxic behaviors of those who try to throw you off your game. Stay vigilant and know that boundaries are set to protect you for a reason.

Today's Affirmation:
I AM BLESSED WITH EVERYTHING I WANT IN LIFE!

Day 35

*"Never lay down twice to give people a second chance
to walk all over you."*

In life those who don't wish us well can sometimes be the people who are the closest to you. Sometimes you have to take a step back to get a better visual. These are usually the individuals who show their true colors when things get rough and real. See who stays grounded and pay attention to who disappears.

Today's Affirmation:

*I AM PROTECTED FROM THOSE WHO
DON'T LIKE ME!*

Day 36

"Learning a lesson gives an opportunity to create a smoother path."

Most of the time we feel we need to be in a certain position to be ready to receive valuable information. Just know and trust that the universe (God) is always talking to us. This may be through an experience, through people, through a movie or even a song. Just know that there is always an opportunity to obtain knowledge, you just have to stay in a mindset of receiving

Today's Affirmation:
MONEY FLOWS TO ME WITH NO EFFORT!

Day 37

"Transparency creates longevity."

Honesty has to start with ourselves. We have to get real about the things we are doing in this lifetime. For something to be transparent you have to be able to see through it. It is important that we keep things real clear with ourselves. That is the only way we can show up for anything within our lives. Whether that is people, our dreams or ambitions.

Today's Affirmation:

I AM THE CREATOR AND ALL MY DREAMS COME TRUE!

Day 38

"Your past does not have to dictate your future."

Please know that this life is about progression. You are not expected to be the same person at twenty-five that you were at eighteen. Just like you are not going to be the same person at forty that you were at thirty. For this reason, why would you still be shaming yourself for something that was done ten to fifteen years ago? You're not even the same person. By the grace of the universe you made a mistake and it helped you grow. If anything, there was a lesson to be learned in that moment and it doesn't define the current you. If anything it made you stronger, it made you better.

Today's Affirmation:
I AM THE BEST VERSION OF MYSELF!

Day 39

"There is always a gift in any bad situation, you just have to find it."

When we are dealing with negative conflict it is hard to see anything beyond what is in front of us. We tend to only focus on the negative aspect of the situation at hand. I encourage you to see the good in the situation. It may be a hard issue, but there's still a blessing attached to it. Whether you see the blessing today, tomorrow or next year, there is one, you just have to find out or wait until it finds you.

Today's Affirmation:
I AM WORTHY OF ALL THE GOOD I WANT IN MY LIFE!

Day 40

*"Planning can make things perfect or imperfect.
Either way, something will be learned."*

Planning is imperative when making a decision or reaching a goal. Although I understand some people are able to cultivate an extensive amount of creativity on the fly, I am also learning there is less stress and minimal correction involved when things are planned out.

Today's Affirmation:
I AM HAPPINESS AND JOY!

Day 41

"A major part of healing from the pain is staying in the present, accepting the past and knowing you will be better in the future."

The best way to heal yourself is to connect with yourself. All the outside influences like alcohol, drugs, social media, porn, food, and sex will only be temporary fixes. The best way to do this is sit with your emotions through meditation, writing, walks in nature, music, or coloring. Revert back to the things that were appealing to you as a child. Once you get through this rough patch during this cycle (because there will be more) you will see how much you elevated. Leveling up is the best revenge and when you come out the healing hiatus your new energy will speak for itself.

Today's Affirmation:
I WILL ALWAYS DO MY BEST!

Day 42

"You have everything you need to believe in yourself even when no one else does."

S ometimes the best thing is to keep your moves in private. Mostly because if your motivation comes from external validation, you're going to constantly be questioning yourself. You have to be your biggest fan and motivator first and foremost. So, if no one agrees with you at least you know you do and that is all that matters.

Today's Affirmation:
I AM HEALTHY AND WEALTHY!

Day 43

"Timing is everything. What is for you will be for you and nothing can change that."

You can't expect a rack of lamb to be cooked at the same time frame as a cup of noodles. The universe has a designated time for everything to occur. Sometimes its immediate, sometimes it can take months maybe even years. Set yourself up to be in a mindset of receiving it, setup your physical environment and your emotional space to know how to keep it. Most of the time when we aren't perseverating on something, and we turn our focus on bettering ourselves the exact thing we have been yearning for shows up unannounced and unexpectedly.

Today's Affirmation:
TODAY EVERYTHING WILL WORK IN MY FAVOR!

Day 44

"Subtracting the negative people from your circle, will create a positive lifestyle."

There are people who surround us and want the best for us and then there are those who have ill intent. Trust yourself to know the difference. If you are manifesting a life full of love and abundance it is going to be hard to make that a reality if there is someone in your presence trying to sabotage that. Let them go. Misery loves company.

Today's Affirmation:
I AM LIVING MY BEST LIFE ALWAYS!

Day 45

"Negative people will always have something negative to say but that has more to do with them and less to do with you."

S ome people make it their life's mission to intentionally hurt people. Typically, this has more to do with them than it does you. Just pray for them and let it go. People who are in a place of understanding who they are will come to their own conclusions about you. And if they don't, oh well, as long as it isn't the person cutting your check.

Today's Affirmation:
I AM ALIVE AND FREE!

Day 46

"Express gratitude for Gods rejection because He saw what you didn't and in turn you were being protected."

Sometimes people leave you out of conversations and situations because they know you will be the center of attention. Don't let their insecurity stop your drive. Keep pushing through and wave at them from the top.

Today's Affirmation:
I ONLY HAVE POSITIVE
EXPECTATIONS!

Day 47

"Never be too arrogant to where you miss opportunities for blessing and lessons."

Everyone in your circle should be at a level that you aspire to be at. Knowledge is power and can never be taken away, make sure you're around people who are seeking it just as much as you are. Everyone you spend time with should be vibrating at elevated levels and if they aren't it's time to find new friends. Not only financially but also mentally and spiritually.

Today's Affirmation:
I AM RECEIVING ALL OF THE
BLESSINGS THE UNIVERSE/GOD HAS
FOR ME!

Day 48

"Never give up or fold. Many people want to see you reach your goals."

S ome people are waiting for you to fold so they can take your place. Other people are watching you because you inspire them. Whatever the case may be, keep pushing!

Today's Affirmation:
I WOKE UP HEALTHY AND WHOLE TODAY!

Day 49

"The real bag is inner peace."

When you think you have everything you want and need, set goals for something bigger. Know that you deserve it all and can have it all. Don't let anyone tell you different, don't allow your thoughts to tell you anything different. Having more in life always starts with being centered in all areas. These areas are spiritual, mental and physical.

Today's Affirmation:

I AM GRATEFUL FOR ALL THE GOOD IN MY LIFE!

Day 50

"Remember that your mess is your message."

Remember that our power comes from the ability to own and accept our past. Understand that our past is not us. It is happening for us and not to us. Once we get into this space it gives us the opportunity to help other people see this as well.

Today's Affirmation:
EVERYTHING I WANT IS
ATTAINABLE!

Day 51

"Some of us spend our entire lives trying to fit in when God made us to stand out."

There is only one you. There is not any person who has exactly what you have and that is a beautiful thing. Embrace it, love it and reside in gratitude to know that God saw it fit for your presence to reside on this earth during this time because you had something to contribute. You are a blessing, know that, feel that and believe it.

Today's Affirmation:

I AM FILLED WITH LOVE, PEACE AND BLESSINGS!

Day 52

*"Don't allow everyone at your table especially if they
keep taking and not contributing to the meal."*

Be aware of individuals who seek
opportunities to always receive and
never have anything to give. It's a
loving action to give to people who are in need
but recognize when someone may be taking
advantage of your kindness. Pay attention to
who you're constantly doing for and then take
the time to think about the times you may need
help. Are those people available to you? You
may need to balance the scale and surround
yourself with those who contribute just as
much as you do in relationship. Because
eventually, you'll find yourself running on E
after you have filled their tank.

Today's Affirmation:
I AM PROTECTED AND CARED FOR
ALWAYS!

Day 53

"Never let the same snake bite you twice."

At some point you have to stop letting the same scenarios and people bother you. You will keep getting triggered by the same situations because people want to create a narrative based on your reaction. Don't give them a story to tell. Walk away and let it go. Keep going about your day as if they don't exist in it.

Today's Affirmation:
I AM BEAUTIFUL INSIDE AND OUT!

Day 54

"A clear mind is a healthy mind."

Research states that the average person has about 12,000 to 60,000 thoughts in one day and about 90 percent of them are critical or negative. Thoughts will come and go naturally but what you think will definitely have an effect on your mind, body and spirit. Make sure you create an awareness of these thoughts and what you are telling yourself. Create healthy loving thoughts to create a healthy loving mind.

Today's Affirmation:
TODAY IS FILLED WITH HAPPINESS
AND PEACE!

Day 55

"Every wave isn't meant to be rode."

Intent is very important behind every thought, action and behavior. When something presents itself but there is some sort of ill intent behind it to where if it were followed through it could potentially hurt you or someone else in the process its best to not do it. The universe is all about balance and for every action there is a reaction. Karma is that act of balancing, make sure you're putting enough good out there to create a good balance for yourself and stay away from any situation that would lead the karma to balancing out in a negative way.

Today's Affirmation:
ALL OF MY DREAMS ARE COMING TRUE!

Day 56

"Today is a new day, starting off fresh, no need to reside in the past, it has already left."

The best gift that comes with waking up in the morning after a bad day is that, that day is over. It's never happening again, and you have been giving an opportunity to start over. To make things different. Take this opportunity to take a deep breath and make this day better than it was yesterday. You get a second chance.

Today's Affirmation:
I CONSCIOUSLY CREATE THE BEAUTIFUL LIFE I DESIRE!

Day 57

"Sometimes you have to let go to show you love yourself more."

S ometimes the hardest thing in love is letting go. But sometimes you have to, especially if you and the other person aren't seeing eye to eye and there is no compromise. It's good to step away from the situation and reset. The parties involved may just be growing apart instead of together and that is okay. Not all relationships have a forever tag on them, in fact, most are for a season and for a specific reason.

Today's Affirmation:
I DON'T TAKE NO FOR AN ANSWER WHEN IT COMES TO MY GOALS!

Day 58

"Resentment is like drinking poison and expecting the other person to die. Just let it go."

Don't let people live rent free in your head. Forgiveness doesn't mean you have to engage in relationship with a person, but it does mean you have to let go of the resentment that is polluting your mind. What happened has happened and it may be the worst possible thing. But letting the anger fester inside of you when the other person is living their life is not going to make you feel better. Take the time today to release the burden and let karma and God take on the weight of that situation.

Today's Affirmation:
I CAN ONLY DO MY BEST ALWAYS!

Day 59

"Clowns will be clowns. It's up to you to stop participating in the circus."

Some people literally argue for fun. But it's very difficult for them to do so if no one is responding. Mostly because they look crazy talking to themselves. Don't feed into nonproductive arguments especially when it is a person who is committed to being right regardless of the content. Usually they are a clown that you will never convince to see things in your light. Let them keep up their circus but stop attending it and giving them the unnecessary attention.

Today's Affirmation:
I AM PRESENT IN EVERY MOMENT!

Day 60

"We are not a copy but an original design, a masterpiece."

Live your life as if you know that and believe that. There is no one here like you. You are needed here on this earth to bring your unique light and to let it shine. We all see it, do you?

Today's Affirmation:
I AM A SPECIAL CONTRIBUTION TO THIS WORLD!

Day 61

"Do not sacrifice your wants and needs for the purpose of pleasing others."

No, is a complete sentence. Use it. If you don't want to go to that party, don't go. If you don't want to help that friend with their bill, don't. If you don't want to keep giving that person a ride because it adds thirty minutes to your commute and you find yourself tired, then stop. If you don't feel comfortable doing something don't do it. If you're hesitant because of what someone else may think of you, you may need to reassess your ability to set boundaries. Boundaries are a very important factor in knowing how to take care of your priorities over others.

Today's Affirmation:
ALL OF THE GOOD IN THE WORLD FLOWS TO ME EASILY!

Day 62

"Life is too short to hold back, say what you mean and mean what you say."

The four agreements mention being impeccable with your word. Sometimes your word is all you have in some situations. Just make sure your being honest and forth coming with that word. It may be difficult in some situations. But in the long run you will be happy that you did.

Today's Affirmation:
MY SUCCESS IN LIFE IS
GUARANTEED!

Day 63

"Numbing out is just a temporary fix, feeling through your body will allow you to move forward through the healing process."

Emotions are a very real part of who we are. We as humans are a physical body, an emotional body, and a spiritual body. All of these components make us who we are. At times, our physical bodies can be hurt, as well as the emotional and spiritual part of us. When this happens at times the emotional pain outweighs the physical pain. When we get in this place, we tend to do things that will make us forget these feelings. But it doesn't really help us in the long run because we are avoiding it. Replacing those feelings with drinking, sex, gambling, and overspending is like putting a Band-Aid over a leaky faucet. In order to feel better long term, allow yourself to feel those sad moments. Don't shame yourself for this process. But also stop running from them and deal with them head on. Once you get this process start to focus on the solution rather than the problem. You can get through this! You got this!

Today's Affirmation:
I ONLY FOCUS ON THE THINGS I CAN CONTROL!

Day 64

"There are no accidents or coincidences."

No one is here by mistake. You are in the right place at the right time. This may be a difficult concept to accept if you are currently struggling. But just understand that if things aren't going right, this moment you're in is meant to teach you something long term. There is hardly in growth in areas of comfort. Know and believe you will come out of whatever it is a new person and better than ever. If you are currently in a good place. Write something you are grateful for and take a moment to smile about it and choose to continue maintaining happiness as long as you can. You deserve it.

Today's Affirmation:
I CAN HANDLE ANYTHING THAT COMES MY WAY!

Day 65

"Do the unexpected, change the game."

Been sitting on an idea but you feel hesitant because it's never been done before? Guess what? It's never been done before because we are waiting for you to jump off the ledge and take that leap. Step outside of fear and do something you have been putting off. Start it today while you are alive and breathing in the present. What do you have to lose?

Today's Affirmation:
MY MIND IS CALM AND CLEAR
THROUGH ALL SITUATIONS!

Day 66

"Always make your next move your best move."

Many times, I have come to a place of reacting out of emotion and instantly felt consumed with guilt. Whether this was a frustrating situation, or schoolwork that was rushed due to anxiety. Things tend to go better when we give ourselves time to carefully plan them out. When we give ourselves time to think before we react? Always think about making every move a well thought out calculated process so that it can be better with every step you take on this life journey.

Today's Affirmation:
I AM ON THE PATH OF ABUNDANCE!

Day 67

"Let the problem go and focus on the solution."

In life there are going to be many disagreements, bad deals, or just frustrating days in general that leave us feeling like we are running on E. Most of the time we feel this way because we are dwelling on what is wrong in the situation rather than thinking how we can fix the situation. Or not wanting to accept the fact that there is really nothing we can do about it. It's okay to allow yourself to feel these emotions. They are natural and they are what make us human, but we aren't supposed to stay in them. Once you give yourself some time to feel the emotions of disappointment, anger and frustration, start making a plan of how you can get yourself out of it.

Today's Affirmation:
I KNOW MY WORTH!

Day 68

"Manifest, be practical, and work smarter not harder."

Think of practical ways to make your day flow. Whether that is asking someone for help, writing a to do list, or even just giving yourself a much-needed break to just rest. Working smarter will definitely minimize the stress that comes with working harder.

Today's Affirmation:
I HAVE EVERYTHING I NEED IN THIS LIFE!

Day 69

"Sometimes just being a good person will never be enough and that is okay."

Reciprocity is not always a guarantee in relationships. Sometimes when you do good deeds out of the kindness of your heart they may not be appreciated or valued by others. But what is most important is that you value them for yourself. Do good deeds because it feels good to you. Not because you expect anything in return. Know that the laws of karma work both ways. You will reap your reward. It's coming.

Today's Affirmation:
I ONLY HAVE GOOD PEOPLE IN MY LIFE!

Day 70

"Visualize what you want and move like it is already yours."

The first area of manifestation comes from the ability to imagine yourself with whatever it is that you want. As a child this was something that was more or less second nature. As we become adult's imagination becomes a lost art. Let's take this time to try it out. Close your eyes, take some deep breaths until your body is completely relaxed. Relax from the crown of your head to the soles of your feet. Now with your eyes closed picture the setting, visualize yourself doing what it is that you want to do or receiving what you want to receive. Put this in your delay practice until you reach your goal.

Today's Affirmation:
I AM BIGGER THAN ANY OF MY PROBLEMS!

Day 71

"Manifest that ish."

Anything you want is within reach. You just simply have to set it in your mind that it is yours. Create a thought for what it is you want. Don't worry about the how initially focus purely on the what. Visualize yourself in that place and watch things fall into place to make that happen. You are only as powerful as you believe you are.

Today's Affirmation:
ALL MY DREAMS ARE BECOMING REALITY!

Day 72

"Make sure the ideals you are projecting are facts and not feelings."

Emotions can be a good thing, but when they aren't, they can rule your day in the most negative way. Emotions can fluctuate solely on the basis of what we tell ourselves. If you are feeling negative emotions from a specific thought. Check in with yourself to make sure those thoughts are actually facts. What you tell yourself is substantially the full basis for how you feel about yourself.

Today's Affirmation:
I AM MENTALLY AND PHYSICALLY HEALTHY!

Day 73

"Don't judge people for the things you have yet to experience."

It's very easy for people to come up with their own perspective about anyone's negative situation. I have been in a place where I thought I had all the answers to what I would do in a situation. The funny thing about that it is that I had the most opinions about situations I had never experienced for myself. I had been very judgmental and critical, thinking I had all of the answers. But interestingly enough once I was in the situation myself, everything I thought I would do went completely out of the window. If you feel very strongly about a situation you have yet to experience take a step back and see yourself in the other person's shoes. Do they need criticism right now? Is being judgmental really going to help the situation? Sometimes people just need a listening ear or a supportive friend.

Just be that person for them, because you never know when you may need the support for yourself.

Today's Affirmation:
I AM RESILIENT!

Day 74

"Understand you were created in the universe's (GOD's) image, there is no need to compare yourself to others."

There is only one you on this earth right now. God believed that this world needed you and what you contribute to this world is unique mostly because it could never be duplicated. Live your life knowing that you are special, and you are here for a reason. Don't ever forget that and walk like you know that.

Today's Affirmation:
I AM AT PEACE WITH EVERYTHING THAT IS HAPPENING IN MY LIFE!

Day 75

"When things are in alignment there is no outside source that will have the power to interrupt that."

What is meant for you is for you. There is nothing anyone can say or do to take that away. And if it does get taken away nine times out of ten, there is something else better waiting for you. You may have noticed in your life that someone or something may be trying to interrupt something that is for you and they fail every time. It's because you are blessed and cared for. So, no need to worry.

Today's Affirmation:
I AM INIFINENTELY LOVED!

Day 76

"Love is in all things; you just have to be ready to receive it."

The most important loving relationship you will have will be the one you engage in with yourself. Through this process you can teach others how to love you by the way they see you loving and taking care of yourself. The only way to receive it, is to first give it to yourself.

Today's Affirmation:
I AM WORTHY!

Day 77

"Love dwells within first."

It is very difficult and almost impossible to love others if you have no love within. How can you give something to someone if you don't feel it yourself? Love has to be an outpouring and overflow of what you already have inside of you. Take some time to love on you so that what you give is an overflow and not a depletion

Today's Affirmation:
I LOVE MYSELF UNCONDITIONALLY!

Day 78

"If you want a different outcome the change has to start with you."

The definition of insanity is doing the same thing over and over and over and expecting the outcome to be different. You want something different you have to change what you are doing. If you want a better job, you can't consistently be late to the current one. If you want to be a better friend maybe write down the steps necessary to be better in those relationships. If you want more money maybe adjust your current spending habits. Anything you want you can have you just have to adjust your current behaviors to be in alignment with what it is that you want.

Today's Affirmation:
I AM EMPOWERED!

Day 79

"Time is priceless, choose what you spend it on wisely, because once it's gone you can't get it back."

You can't put any monetary value on time and once it's done its gone. So, try to do things that don't put you in a place of wasting it or even worse regretting it. Call that person and talk to them if you miss them. Take that chance and apply for that job, tell that person you love them, spend extra time with your children or other family members. Because once the time is gone all you have are the memories.

Today's Affirmation:
I HAVE EVERYTHING IT TAKES TO
SUCCEED!

Day 80

"Live and love life without regrets."

U nderstand that whatever has happened in the past cannot be changed. You can make things right if you have wronged people, but the actions cannot be changed. It is important that you don't shame yourself for it. Who you were yesterday is not who you are today or last year or ten years ago? Through this life as long as we are breathing there is space and opportunity to grow from all situations. Live your life learning from mistakes and take the time to grow from them. Enjoy life as much as you can, it's very short.

Today's Affirmation:
I AM DESTINED FOR GREATNESS!

Day 81

"Anyone's story can start over again, it's up to you to create a new chapter."

Every day is a new opportunity to change things you don't like in your life. Waking up has given you another chance to shift gears and change your journey. Take the time and opportunity to change your path. If you don't like the way things are going you have the time and space to change it. Life is too short to just be treading through the days. Live it to the fullest because the time is too short to be unhappy.

Today's Affirmation:
I LOVE MYSELF FOR WHO I AM!

Day 82

"Blood does not make everyone your family."

Because someone is related by blood it does not give them the opportunity to treat you any type of way. That goes for a mother, grandmother, dad, brother, sister, auntie or cousin. If someone is being abusive or negative towards you protect your energy and set boundaries. Let them know that it isn't okay and keep your distance from them if they never put in the effort to learn how to respect you and love you.

Today's Affirmation:
I NEVER GIVE UP!

Day 83

"Fear is ultimately an illusion created in our minds (F)alse (E)vidence (A)ppearing (R)eal."

Fear is an important emotion to keep us safe, but it can also be a culprit in preventing us from living our full lives. Don't allow fear to put you in a place of living life in a small box. Don't allow fear to be little your hopes, dreams and desires. Know the difference between the fear that is protecting you in a dark alley or the fear that is created through negative thoughts and emotions.

Today's Affirmation:
TODAY IS A GOOD DAY!

Day 84

"Stop giving people the benefit of doubt, it ultimately gives them permission to believe words over a track record of hurtful actions."

Whomever came up with the phrase "benefit of doubt" didn't really trust themselves, their vision or their intuition. When people show you who they are believe them the first time and act accordingly.

Today's Affirmation:
I TRUST MY GIFT OF DISCERNMENT!

Day 85

"Bad days only last twenty-four hours but good support and friendships can last a lifetime."

You are only as solid as the team you surround yourself with. Naturally the universe aligns us with those in our soul group to help us along our journey. These people come in the form of teachers, coaches, parents, siblings, friends etc. Check in with your team and let them know why you appreciate them today.

Today's Affirmation:
I ALWAYS MAKE SOMETHING HAPPEN!

Day 86

"Sometimes soaring like an eagle requires you to leave the flock behind."

When you choose to elevate in life everyone can't come with you. Life is a journey full of relationships, and not all of them are meant to last forever. If you are finding that the relationships you have are keeping you stuck in a place with little to no progression now is the time to evaluate. Some people may have to get left and that is okay. It just means that relationship served its purpose. You will know when it gets to that point. Because it feels more difficult to maintain than it would to let it go. That means it's time to walk away.

Today's Affirmation:
I DON'T LET HATERS TAKE MY ENERGY!

Day 87

"The love you have for others should come from an overflow of love that you already have for yourself."

Whether you are a daughter, son, sister, brother, mother, or father before you can be any of those roles you have to make sure you have enough energy to be enough for you. If your tank is running on E there is not enough gas to show up for these other roles. Make sure you take care of you first so that you can show up for the people you love.

Today's Affirmation:
I AM VALUABLE IN ALL WAYS!

Day 88

"Bees don't explain to flies why it is better to land on flowers than it is to land on shit."

Sometimes you have to let people go through their own journeys. We may have been down the same road and know that they are headed down the block of barbed wire and detours. We can tell them 'til they are blue in the face. But they want to experience it for themselves. All we can do is love them in the process and release codependency and set boundaries if necessary. A lot of time unconditional love can be letting go rather than struggling to hold on.

Today's Affirmation:
EVERY DAY I AM CLOSER TO
MEETING MY GOALS!

Day 89

"Remember that roots grow underground before they can bloom under the sun."

Sometimes we have to hit rock bottom before we can reach our level of greatness. Most of the time if we are lucky this life doesn't give us short cuts. We get into a place of struggle and hard times, but all of these situations are built to create solid foundations and the roots necessary to create nourishment for our souls.

Today's Affirmation:
I AM STRONGER EVERY DAY!

Day 90

"Stop killing your dreams before they even leave your thoughts."

Ever had a great idea and then killed it in a matter of minutes with 100 reasons why you think it wouldn't work? But couldn't you think of 100 ideas as to why it would work? What is the difference? Why do you go to the negative before the positive? Do something different today. When you have a negative thought? Acknowledge it and then counter it with the exact opposite. Whether you have a clear plan or not. Choose the great thoughts over the thoughts of failing. No one will believe in you like you. But it starts with your thoughts.

Today's Affirmation:
I AM WORTHY OF UNREQUITED
LOVE!

Day 91

*"What irritates us about others is usually something
we despise in ourselves."*

Have you ever been in a place and seen someone who made you cringe? Cringe because they were judging everyone in the room. Your thoughts spiral into who does he think he is or who does she think she is, to judge anyone. Just to realize you were judging them for being judgmental. Remember before you find fault in others take the plank out your own eye.

Today's Affirmation:
ANYTHING THAT ISN'T FOR ME FALLS OFF NATURALLY!

Day 92

"Don't be afraid to shine alone, the sun, moon and stars do it day and night without missing a beat."

One fact about life is that you're born alone, and you die alone. In between time you tend to come full circle with getting to know yourself, loving yourself and finding ways to make that time with you enjoyable. The quicker you come to this place of acceptance of self the easier the journey will be. Because the relationship you have with you is the only thing in this life you can fully control and change at any point. Take your time and make the most of the time you spend with yourself.

Today's Affirmation:
I AM POWERFUL!

Day 93

Fill up your tank.

G rand rising,

Before getting your day started write down five positive things you have experienced so far this year. Also write down five not so positive things you have experienced this year. Reflect on how they have changed you as a person. Reflect on how they forced you to grow.

Today's Affirmation:
I MAKE THINGS HAPPEN!

Day 94

"Protect your energy at all cost."

We are all filled with energy. Some put in a conscious effort to keep their energy vibration at a high frequency. Unfortunately, there are some people who because they aren't able to achieve this feat, they tend to bring you down to their low levels. Remember misery loves company. When someone is clearly having a rough time and they begin to project their issues on you, disengage in that interaction. It's not worth it, walk away and protect your peace. Don't allow them to drain you.

Today's Affirmation:
I AM IN THE RIGHT PLACE AT THE RIGHT TIME!

Day 95

"Life is a game and there are levels to this ish."

C urve balls are always going to be thrown in this game of life. We already know that. The bigger question is what will you do when they come. No matter how things or circumstances may lift you up its almost certain there will be something to bring you down. Don't let it keep you there. Put your trust in something healthy to bring yourself out of it. Whether that is a trusted friend, a useful tool like meditation or writing, maybe even a therapist or something as extreme as letting out a loud scream. Whatever you need to do, just do it. Focus on the solution and release the problem. There are levels to this ish and as long as your breathing keep leveling up.

Today's Affirmation:
I AM PROUD OF MYSELF TODAY!

Day 96

Fill up your tank.

G rand rising,

Before you start your day, stand in front of your mirror and do this mirror meditation. What is a mirror meditation? I am so glad you asked. Simply stand in front of your mirror, look at yourself in the eyes, take a few breaths and simply tell yourself (by your name of course) I love you. Do these five times and see how you feel. If you don't feel anything, do this every day until you believe it.

Today's Affirmation:
EVERYTHING I NEED IS WITHIN ME!

Day 97

"Forgive but don't forget."

Many of us have had some sort of negative interaction with a human within our lifetime. This could be family, coworkers or even a complete stranger. The opposite of forgiveness is resentment. Holding a grudge inside of you for whatever that person has done to you. Put in a conscious effort to release that from your mind, body and spirit. Because harboring resentment inside your mind, body and spirit is like drinking poison and expecting the other person to die. Although you release the resentful tie you hold with this person it does not automatically require interaction with them. Because you forgive them the interaction in itself that hurt was meant to be a lesson. Once you burn yourself with fire you don't test it out again. Take the lesson, release the resentment and remember it's your choice to decide whether you want to have an interaction with them again. Because you choosing not to is always an option.

Today's Affirmation:
YOU HANDLE YOUR BUSINESS WITH LITTLE EFFORT!

Day 98

"Don't give people an opportunity to fool you a second time."

In a nutshell, if you know your cousin Ray Ray owes everybody in the family twenty-dollars and you don't have it to give freely, please don't give Ray twenty-dollars. If you know Auntie Lucy has had two DUIs and her license is suspended do not let her borrow your car. Don't follow an individual's words, pay attention their actions. Because if you give them opportunity to mess up a second time and it is something that directly affects you, that is no longer their problem it is now yours. Once someone shows you who they are believe them.

Today's Affirmation:
I CHOOSE TO BE THE BEST VERSION OF ME!

Day 99

"It's good to treat people how you want to be treated but don't allow them to abuse it."

It's a blessing to be a blessing in the lives of others. When this is done with pure intentions most of the time you find people who are appreciative of your loving actions. However, there are some people who don't quite understand love and can be in a place of abusing it. It is up to the giver to be in a place of loving themselves first by setting boundaries. Don't let greedy mongers take you out of having a loving heart. Call them out on their BS and continue to spread it to those who don't drain you and show appreciation.

Today's Affirmation:
I WILL ATTRACT JOY AND
HAPPINESS TODAY!

Day 100

"The only people who don't like boundaries are those benefitting from you not having any."

Having boundaries is one of the truest forms of self-love. Boundaries provide you with an opportunity to consciously choose yourself first. Many have viewed this concept erroneously as selfish or self-centered. There will be times where things are indeed compromised but should never be at the expense of your own happiness and health. If you aren't giving restrictions to others in your life in attempt to keep some of that energy for yourself, you won't have anything left to give or you will give out of emptiness. Life is too short for that. Keep your cup full so that it can be a blessing to others.

Today's Affirmation:
I AM BUILT TO TAKE ON WHATEVER COMES MY WAY!

Day 101

"Face your fears head on or you will spend the rest of your life running from them."

Some of the deepest parts of our character are not exposed to those around us or we keep them suppressed in fear of what others may think. This in turn could lead us to operating in a safe space of living life without risk. With little risk comes little reward. What fears are holding you from reaching your fullest potential.? Write them out and release them. Consciously choose to let them go. Your life journey will be much lighter without them.

Today's Affirmation:
I AM COURAGEOUS TODAY!

Day 102

"There is a reason the flight attendant says place your oxygen mask on first, know that it is imperative that you take care of you first."

Make sure you consciously take some time out to care for yourself. Whether your role is a boss, an employee, mother, father, son, daughter etc., if your mental, spiritual and physical health aren't in alignment it will be very difficult for you to show up and be fully present in any of these roles. Make sure you're checking in with yourself the way you check in with everyone else.

Today's Affirmation:
I AM BRAVE ENOUGH TO SPEAK MY TRUTH!

Day 103

"Holding a grudge towards someone who could care less is a waste of time, leave the beefing up to Ruth Chris."

Stop letting people live rent free in your head. If you were able to dismiss the person from your life due to the connection being toxic look at the glass as half full. Stop letting people who are no longer present in your reality affect your day to day. Forgive the situation but don't forget and remember it is much healthier to let ago than to allow your past to haunt you regularly. How will you move on with a better, brighter future? The best revenge is not your paper its your peace of mind.

Today's Affirmation:
I AM GROUNDED!

Day 104

"The grass is greener where you water it."

What did you think I would say? Greener on the other side? This may be true but its only true because they water it. Take care of what is yours. Nothing worth having will come easy. There will be hiccups and nothing is perfect. Care for relationships, things and yourself with a loving intention and watch all of those situations bloom and flourish.

Today's Affirmation:
I AM WEALTHY!

Day 105

"Make decisions based on character not verbal content."

The quote actions speak louder than words hold a lot of weight when it comes to viewing character. Character is on the basis of how you operate as a human in this world. How you intentionally treat other people whether the world is looking or not. Anyone can say anything; the ability to communicate with words is a gift. However, they are just that: only words. Make sure your actions reflect what your mouth states. Make sure your words match your actions. You receive what you put out into this world. So be the person you want to be reflected back to you and treat people how you want to be treated not just with words but with actions.

Today's Affirmation:
I AM BRAVE AND BOLD!

Day 106

*"Just because they are your family it doesn't mean
their acceptance or lack thereof validates your worth."*

Your worth isn't defined by anyone but
yourself. Don't allow external
relationships or material things to
allow you to forget that. You are who you say
and believe you are. So, what are you telling
yourself?

Today's Affirmation:
I AM HEALTHY AND STRONG!

Day 107

"Favor isn't fair."

Favor is defined as approval, support or liking for someone or something. Sometimes miracles come to us with no explanation or timing. They just happen because they are for us. Keep believing they are for you and they will continue to happen. Don't stop believing.

Today's Affirmation:
I AM HAPPY AND CONTENT WITH MY LIFE!

Day 108

"Everything you have right now in the present outweighs everything you think you're missing."

There is always something to be grateful for. Just take the time to pull it out. It's very hard to focus when things aren't going right. But even the little things can breathe life into making us crawl out the dark and back into the light. Whether it's the ability to see, having somewhere to sleep, something to eat etc. Also keep in mind that these dark times occur for our benefit as well. They create resilience and strength. Just don't quit. You got this!

Today's Affirmation:
I AM FEARLESS!

Day 109

"Once you perfect loosing there isn't anything that could stop you from winning."

There are no losses in life. Losses is a synonym for lesson. When something doesn't go the way, you think it should or how expected take the time to evaluate the outcome and try again. Because of you have been through this before you now have experience and it puts you a step ahead of where you were before. You got this!

Today's Affirmation:
I HAVE EVERYTHING I NEED TO MAKE TODAY GREAT!

Day 110

"Don't take disrespect, take cash, check, apple pay, and credit cards."

Life is too short to make excuses for abusive behavior. Don't allow anyone to treat you less than what God knows you are worth. That goes for anyone. Relative, associate or boss. Know your worth by not allowing them to treat you any less.

Today's Affirmation:
I AM CONFIDENT!

Day 111

"A wise man knows that a wise man knows nothing."

As long as you are living there is always something to learn or experience. Through this experience is where we develop knowledge and wisdom. Keep an open mind and understand that through learning you grow and develop in seeing your dreams as a reality. Keep dreaming, keep learning.

Today's Affirmation:
I AM WORTHY OF ALL THE GOOD THINGS!

Day 112

"Allow your pain to fuel your passion."

Life is not always about love and light. Those are definitely the good parts of it, but pain and sadness bring out the areas of growth the most. Feel your pain and sadness but don't allow it to keep you in the same space. Use it as the gas needed for you to grow. You may not understand when you're in it but stay the course and you will see it all makes sense in the end. Keep going! don't quit!

Today's Affirmation:
I HAVE THE POWER TO CREATE THE LIFE I WANT!

Day 113

"Vulnerability and honesty are some of the strongest characteristics one can possess."

Although this is true, they are also some of the hardest to express. If you have experienced a lot of hurt in life where people haven't always been trustworthy or transparent it may allow you to put up a wall. When this wall is up it makes it difficult to let anyone in which in turn makes love a very shallow feeling rather than the deep meaning it is intended to have. Get into a space to trust your discernment and understand that the universe is on your side.

Today's Affirmation:
I AM OPEN TO RECEIVING ALL MY BLESSINGS!

Day 114

"Don't allow social media to cloud your perception of real-world success."

Social media allows for three to four minute reels and videos into one's life. Understand that this is not your competition. Allow these things to be motivation rather than the standard. Don't allow a small glimpse into someone's internet reality to put you in a space of shame and guilt. Set goals for yourself without seeking the approval of others.

Today's Affirmation:
I TRUST MYSELF TODAY!

Day 115

"Never forget that a diamond is a piece of coal that just so happen to do well under pressure."

P ressure makes diamonds. Without it they don't exist. Understand that whatever you're going through will have a beautiful outcome in the end. Change your outlook on the situation and visualize the light at the other end of the tunnel.

Today's Affirmation:
I HAVE SPACE IN MY LIFE FOR THE THINGS THAT NOURISH ME!

Day 116

"When you find your calling make sure you're in a place of accepting it."

A lot of the times we are in a place of always finding an end goal. Instead of enjoying the process. The process is the area that you can find the most happiness in. So, although things may not be where you want them to be. Set up the areas in your life that can prepare you once you get there. Something as minimum as a business plan, Financial plan or even just writing a goal. Don't give up!

Today's Affirmation:
I CAN EASILY AFFORD EVERYTHING
I DESIRE!

Day 117

"You cannot navigate your path forward if you keep looking back."

Your past does not define you. There is nothing you can do to change it. But no matter how you view it you have the opportunity every morning to leave it where it is. Don't allow it to determine your future. If you want a clean slate just remember you have one every morning you wake up.

Today's Affirmation:
I AM WORTHY OF ALL THAT I DESIRE!

Day 118

"Hope and pray for wins but most importantly expect them."

Your thoughts create your reality. The negative thoughts that occur after you have created a goal are not your own. Don't let them deter you from the greatness you are destined to be. Acknowledge them and then counter them with the reality you wish to create.

Today's Affirmation:
MY SUCCESS IS GUARANTEED!

Day 119

Fill up your tank.

Before you leave out the door or get your day started write down five things that you want to do as a hobby before the year is up. Pick two and plan out how you can complete them. If you already have a set of hobbies, reflect on how you can make time for them, maybe possibly expanding them or how you could maybe share your craft with the world by either putting it on display or sharing your knowledge with someone who may be interested.

Today's Affirmation:
I AM WILLING TO LET LOVE IN!

Day 120

Fill up your tank.

Grand rising beautiful souls!

Start your day off by simply telling someone you love them. Call them or tell them in person. If you're not in a place of doing that, express your love to a pet, to a plant or find a mirror and tell yourself. Bless someone with your loving energy today.

Today's Affirmation:
ALL MY DESIRES WILL BE MET TODAY!

Day 121

Fill up your tank.

Grand rising beautiful souls!

You have time for a quick gratitude list? How about writing five things you're grateful for. If you can't get to five right away take the time today to work up to it. Think of something you are grateful for as you go throughout your day. As soon as you think about it write it down.

Today's Affirmation:
I HAVE UNIQUE AND AMAZING GIFTS!

Day 122

"Don't leave room for anyone to disturb your peace."

Protect your space and peace at all costs. Do not allow people who are miserable to have opportunities or attempts to bring you down to their level. Stay aware and avoid these people at all costs. Peace is more valuable than money, treat it like you know that.

Today's Affirmation:
I AM IRREPLACABLE!

Day 123

"Perfection is an illusion."

If we were all perfect, there would be no room to be ourselves. No one in this world exudes perfection. What is perfection? Everyone has bad days; everyone has good days and plenty of us have sad days. This goes for the rich, poor, healthy and unhealthy. Stay true in self-discovery and know that your perfection is in your imperfections. It makes you, you and there is no one on this earth like you. That in itself is a beautiful thing, so act accordingly.

Today's Affirmation:
I AM NEEDED IN THIS WORLD!

Day 124

"Do everything with good intention from the heart."

E verything we do is on the basis of our intentions. When we do things from the heart out of love, we find that we get something back from that. When things occur out of obligation we tend to develop resentment. Make sure when you're doing things you check in with yourself to make sure you're in a place of giving and receiving love. Do things because you want to, not because you feel like you have to.

Today's Affirmation:
I DESERVE TO LIVE MY DREAMS!

Day 125

"Forgive those with hurt and hate in their hearts but never forget who they are."

Forgiveness is for you, not the other person. It is a release of anger, shame and resentment. Free yourself from these burdens. However, because you have released these feelings does not mean that you go back to the person that caused the pain in the first place. Forgive and forget. Don't go back picking up the poison leave them where you left them.

Today's Affirmation:
I WILL OPERATE OUTSIDE MY
COMFORT ZONE!

Day 126

"Knowledge is fundamental to mental, spiritual, and physical growth, and is one of the few things that can't be taken away."

If you wake up and you're alert and still breathing that means, there is something to learn. Use that time as opportunity for growth and development. Also keep an open mind and know that you can learn from anyone and everything.

Today's Affirmation:
I WILL WIN!

Day 127

"Bad days will happen but they only last twenty-four hours."

Every day is a new opportunity to do something different. Don't allow yesterday's problems to give you permission to waste the present days' time. It's okay to take time to feel your feelings but only for a moment. Get up and get something done for yourself. You got this!

Today's Affirmation:
I AM LIVING MY BEST LIFE!

Day 128

*"Patience is hard to come by so don't allow low
vibrations to cause you to lose it."*

Choose your battles wisely. There are
people who are just in a place of not
understanding anything other than
themselves. Just let them be. Don't allow their
miserable life and low vibrational behavior to
bring you down to their level. Dismiss them
and leave them where they had you messed up.

Today's Affirmation:
ALL OF LIFES EXPERIENCES ARE
WORKING IN MY FAVOR!

Day 129

"Love like you have never been heart broken."

This can be a difficult task. Being in love causes you to be wide open. This puts you in a place of vulnerability and when things pan out different then the intended expectations it puts you in a space of fear. Fear of being hurt, abandoned or losing the love in general. Whenever you have gone through this know that the love for yourself should override all the love you are surrounded by. Once this cup is full a heart break is something you can fully bounce back from. Don't let those past situations make you miss your future blessing.

Today's Affirmation:
MY PASSIONS FUEL MY PURPOSE!

Day 130

*"The blind leading the blind shows that you should
never allow anyone without a clear vision to lead you."*

Y ou will only go as far as the company
you keep. Look at your circle and see if
they match your goals and desires. Also
do you have a mentor who has the knowledge
of the goals you are trying to achieve. Maybe
it's time to go to the drawing board. We
outgrow people all of the time. Understand
some relationships are meant to last a lifetime
some are just for a reason and a season. Act
accordingly and start cleaning house!

Today's Affirmation:
I AM USEFUL IN EVERYTHING I DO!

Day 131

"You are beautiful inside and out without a shred of doubt."

Know that! Exude that. Look in the mirror and tell yourself that you are that one and believe it. Every mirror you see today as you walk past tell yourself that you are that one and the two inside and out. Don't forget it and don't let anyone tell you different.

Today's Affirmation:
I AM AMAZING AND CAN DO ANYTHING I SET MY MIND TO!

Day 132

"Never forget to pour into yourself the way you pour into others."

Don't let these moochers drain your cup. You spend too much time being you. Getting your money, researching new ways to improve your life and just being the ish overall. Don't allow people who do very little to sip from your cup. Don't let them come to your table unless they have something to bring.

Today's Affirmation:
MY LIFE FLOWS WITH BLESSINGS AND OPPORTUNITIES!

Day 133

"Remember the past is gone, the future isn't guaranteed, all we have is the present. Treat it like a gift."

All we have is today. The past is gone the future hasn't happen. So, all we have is today. What are you going to do with it? Sit here focusing on what could have been different? It's already done. So, what now? Worry about what's going to happen? It hasn't even happened yet. So just focus on the now, the only thing that is in your control.

Today's Affirmation:
I ACCEPT WHO I AM FULLY!

Day 134

"Live in your truth, some will like it, and some won't, but it's your life to live not theirs."

Advice is a good thing when it is warranted or from a loving place. But a lot of the time you will find people projecting their own experiences which have nothing to do with you. Take and leave what you want but your decisions on your life are truly yours and you don't have to apologize for it. Stay true to yourself and trust yourself.

Today's Affirmation:
I DESERVE HAPPINESS!

Day 135

"It's not a walk in the park when you keep letting toxic people slide."

Boundaries are for you not for others. Boundaries are important because they allow you to be in control of your life on your terms. This prevents allowing abusive and toxic people to run rampant in your reality and or your thoughts. Set boundaries once these people reveal their ugly ways.

Today's Affirmation:
I ONLY ATTRACT GOOD PEOPLE IN MY LIFE!

Day 136

"Don't worry about the people God removed from your life. He heard conversations you didn't, saw things you couldn't and made moves you wouldn't."

Let go and let be. People are meant for seasons and reasons. Some may not outlast certain periods of times. That is fine, life moves on and you can too. Focus on your own decisions and be grateful that God cleared space for you to focus on the healthy relationships in your life.

Today's Affirmation:
I FORGIVE MYSELF FOR MY
SHORTCOMINGS!

Day 137

"Abundance and prosperity are not always developed through struggle but when it is it definitely creates gratitude."

When you have worked hard for something it's not just the award or the end goal you have to be proud of, be proud of the process. The ups and downs. It makes the reward mean so much more.

Today's Affirmation:
I AM THE BEST VERSION OF MYSELF!

Day 138

"Be you, be brave, be confident in everything you do."

Life is too short to not be your true self. Also, you are depriving people of the blessing that comes when they encounter you. Allow people the opportunity to get to know the authentic you, the brave, the confident you. Remember there is only you and although others may try you can never be duplicated.

Today's Affirmation:
MY COMMITMENT TO MYSELF IS
REAL!

Day 139

"Worry about nothing, pray about everything."

Worrying and overthinking is a waste of time. It doesn't change anything. It just messes with your mind and steals your happiness. Never force anything. Just let it be. If it's meant to be, it will be. And if it doesn't happen consider it a blessing you were saved from.

Today's Affirmation:
I AM NOT MY MISTAKES!

Day 140

"Stop letting people turn you into who they want you to be and just be who God made you to be."

Be yourself and the right people will love the real you and the ones who don't, don't deserve to anyway. Leave them where they are. You only want to be surrounded by the people who love and want the best for you. Tell the haters bye.

Today's Affirmation:

I ACCEPT MY SELF FULLY!

Day 141

"Be so determined to learn that you become unstoppable."

Life is full of lessons and the majority of those lessons come from the people in our lives. Not all of the lessons are good ones. Don't allow them to repeat. Accept these people for who they are but set firm boundaries to protect your peace.

Today's Affirmation:
LIFE GIVES ME ABUNDANT
BLESSINGS!

Day 142

"Treat people how you want to be treated."

You never know what someone is dealing with behind closed doors. No matter how happy someone looks, how loud their laugh is, there still can be a level of hurt that is indescribable. So be kind. Even when others or not, choose to be kind.

Today's Affirmation:
I AM RESPECTED FOR JUST BEING ME!

Day 143

"Loyalty is different from love. Just because someone loves you it does not mean they are loyal to you."

L oyalty is defined as a strong allegiance towards a person or concept. There are plenty of people who can show you love but to have loyalty requires a commitment that most don't have. Don't get the two confused because one does not guarantee the other. Loyalty is rare and should start off with you being loyal to yourself first and foremost.

Today's Affirmation:
I MAKE THINGS HAPPEN!

Day 144

"Let go of anything that doesn't make you happy."

In other words, let that ish go. When you get to a point of elevation in life, time wasted is not productive to money or happiness. Any negativity or moochers need to get left where you found it. We are trying to live a productive abundant life rich in peace, health, love and happiness and everyone and everything cannot go, or they will make the journey much harder than it has to be.

Today's Affirmation:
I AM SURROUNDED BY POSITIVITY!

Day 145

"It isn't the burden or weight of the problem it is how you navigate or carry the solution."

Don't underestimate your power when you are faced with a problem. If you can deal with a problem you are more than capable of developing the right solution. Don't doubt yourself. You are more than capable and have everything you need.

Today's Affirmation:
I AM IMPORTANT!

Day 146

"Some people don't like you just because your strength reminds them of their weakness. Don't let the hate slow you down."

Not everyone is running the same race and that is okay. Often times the people we start off with we have to leave behind because they just aren't able to keep up. A lot of people aren't going to be happy with your decision to remove them from your life and their hate may be a consequence of that because they don't have anything better to do with themselves.

Today's Affirmation:

I ATTRACT HONEST PEOPLE IN MY LIFE!

Day 147

"Be thankful for discernment. It is equivalent to seeing the truth through God's eyes."

Through life experience I have learned that your worse enemy could be the closest person to you. Typically, you get red flags from the beginning and choose to dismiss them in attempt to give people chances they don't deserve. Protect your energy and let the haters do what they do best. Waste their time hating while you're getting to it.

Today's Affirmation:
IT'S OKAY TO FEEL YOUR FEELINGS!

Day 148

"They apologize when you find out, but they are not sorry when you don't know."

Be cautious of people who don't have your best interest at heart. People who love you will keep it real with you no matter how hard it is. Be wary of the people around you who become the audience to those who are talking mess about you. Cut those relationships off.

Today's Affirmation:

EVERY DAY IS A NEW DAY FILLED WITH HAPPINESS!

Day 149

"Recognize you have always been a star, when will you allow yourself to shine?"

You being a beautiful special individual is not based on the things you have or haven't done. It is not based on the things you have or do not have. It is simple based on you just being you. You have everything you need to live the life you want to live today. Manifestation comes with a simple idea in knowing it can happen for you. Believe in yourself the way you cheer and believe in everyone else.

Today's Affirmation:
I ALWAYS DO BETTER THAN I DID YESTERDAY!

Day 150

"Quality friendships over quantity always."

Everyone wants to cultivate friendships and relationships that have balance. If you find yourself constantly giving and never receiving, it's time to take a look at those situations. You deserve just as much love as you put out plus some. Don't allow anyone's actions or behaviors make you think anything differently.

Today's Affirmation:

I CHOOSE TO FOCUS ON THE POSITVE TODAY!

Day 151

"Don't dwell on who let you down, cherish those who hold you up."

The past is in the past for a reason. Let it go and give your energy to those who are in your present.

Today's Affirmation:
I LET GO OF THE NEGATIVE FEELINGS ABOUT MYSELF!

Day 152

"Opinions are like buttholes; everyone has one but 99% of them are full of ish."

S ometimes it's best to make moves in silence. Everyone is not going to agree with your ideas or concepts. In addition to the fact that everyone will have an opinion. Don't allow opinions to sway you from your dreams.

Today's Affirmation:
I KNOW EACH DAY IS A BLESSING
AND A GIFT!

Day 153

"The best relationship you can cultivate is the one you have with yourself first."

Would you date yourself? If so why? If not, Why not? Make sure you are being to yourself what you expect in others. People are only supposed to add to your happiness, not make it.

Today's Affirmation:
I AM CALM AND RELAXED IN EVERY SITUATION!

Day 154

"Life does not have to be perfect to be wonderful."

G ratitude is the best way for blessings to flow. When you're in a place of appreciating what you have the more your blessings appreciate. Life is always what you make it.

Today's Affirmation:
I AM ABUNDANT IN EVERYTHING I DO!

Day 155

"Good things come to those who want something so bad they can't sit still, not to those who wait."

Faith without works is dead. A goal is only a goal until it becomes a reality. However, this reality doesn't just fall from the sky. You have to put yourself in positions to receive them. This can be through conversation and this can be through action. Just get up and make it happen.

Today's Affirmation:
I HAVE PURPOSE!

Day 156

"Stop striving to become a duplicate when God saw fit for you to be the original blueprint."

We are all made in Gods image. God's image makes us perfect because we are an original. We are unique because there is something about us that no one else has. Love yourself for that reason alone.

Today's Affirmation:
I HAVE THE POWER TO DEFEAT MY FEARS!

Day 157

"Those who have experienced severe grief have a true appreciation for authentic happiness."

There are moments in life that cause us great sadness, but it definitely opens our eyes to everything we have in our lives to be grateful for. When times are difficult, and you are consumed with sadness use gratitude as a way to get out of your rut. This too shall pass.

Today's Affirmation:
I AM SURE OF WHO I AM!

Day 158

"Stop dragging your past forward."

Most of the time the journey is slowly progressing because of the baggage being carried. The good thing about the past is that you can choose not to relive it. Let it go and move forward. You can give yourself a second chance even if others won't.

Today's Affirmation:
I TRUST MYSELF!

Day 159

"Your presence is a present. It is a gift."

Don't allow anyone to take advantage of your energy. You just showing up is enough and should be validated as such. Know who you are and most importantly know your worth.

Today's Affirmation:
I AM ROYALTY!

Day 160

"Happiness isn't a destination, it's a state of mind."

Every time you wake up in the morning you are given the opportunity to choose happiness. This may be hard if your thoughts are telling you something different. If it doesn't work today just try again tomorrow. Be gentle with yourself.

Today's Affirmation:
I AM STRONG!

Day 161

"Be cautious of those you think are praying for you but are actually preying on you."

I ntuition does not lie. That gut feeling is a real thing. If you are in the presence of somebody and it doesn't quite feel right, trust yourself. Most of the time these feelings give way to help us avoid the potential hurt that often occurs when dealing with hurt people.

Today's Affirmation:
I LOVE ME!

Day 162

"You can forgive the mistake but never forget the lesson."

Life is all about choices. Initially we feel as though they didn't work in our favor. But most of the time they were situations that occurred to teach us something. A lot of time when we focus on what was taught it makes the healing process easier. Be gentle with yourself.

Today's Affirmation:
I TAKE CARE OF ME!

Day 163

"Give your focus to the intention instead of worrying about the outcome."

People pleasing can be one hell of a drug. Don't get addicted. When we get into those spaces we tend to forget why we are doing what we are doing in the first place. Do something because you love it not because you are hoping to get recognition and pay out of it. Those are good outcomes but should never be the sole purpose.

Today's Affirmation:
I HAVE UNLIMITED POTENTIAL!

Day 164

"Choices are a true indicator of a person's character."

Understand that moral character can make or break you. Your reputation, your relationships and sometimes even your soul. Understand the laws of karma are real and those who move with good intentions tend to reap the benefits of a fruitful life. The symptom of your choices will show up in your harvest.

Today's Affirmation:
I AM INTELLIGENT!

Day 165

"Don't judge others on their present because you have forgotten about your past."

Everyone makes mistakes and we are not excluded from that. Make sure your track record is squeaky clean before you make someone feel less than for theirs. Be a supportive friend not a judgmental hater. You never know when you may be in need.

Today's Affirmation:
I AM WORTHY OF LOVE!

Day 166

"Don't fall for words when we know that actions speak louder."

If a person apologizes and consistently shows the same behavior it means you're holding on to words rather than paying attention to their actions. You deserve more then what they are showing your right now. Move accordingly. Move based on action stop being wavered by empty promises.

Today's Affirmation:
I AM FAITHFUL TO MYSELF!

Day 167

"Don't allow past pain and trauma to make you think you aren't worthy of joy and happiness."

The past is exactly where you left it and it is definitely not a reflection of your worth. If anything, it made you bigger and better.

Today's Affirmation:
I AM NOT MY PAST!

Day 168

"Understand that people will only be as nice and caring towards you as they are to themselves."

Most of the time when people treat you maliciously it typically is a reflection of what they think of themselves. It has nothing to do with you especially if it is occurring for no reason. Just pray for them.

Today's Affirmation:
I AM IN CONTROL OF MY THOUGHTS!

Day 169

"Prayer should not only come with tragedy, remember to also pray and manifest when you are in moments of happiness and peace as well."

Prayer is a talk with God. Not a means of spiritual 911. Speak to God when you don't need anything and see how the blessings will still continue.

Today's Affirmation:
I AM WEALTHY IN ABUNDANCE!

Day 170

"Falling in love can keep you in a place of stagnation or propel you forward, make sure your love is cultivated with the right person."

People only love at their own level of understanding. Most of this comes from their upbringing. Not everyone's love will vibrate on the same frequency as you and that is okay. Find the one that is on the same level as you

Today's Affirmation:
I AM LOVE!

Day 171

"You have to be in a place of enjoying your own company, how can anyone like being with you if you haven't first learned to be with yourself."

Alone time is needed to get acquainted with the most important person in your life. You. For some of us with busy lives and families it makes this such a difficulty feat. But whenever the opportunity presents itself have that *me* time. It's good for the soul and you deserve it.

Today's Affirmation:
I HAVE AN OPEN HEART!

Day 172

"What is for you is for you, it never has to be forced."

There are certain things in this life that are specific to you. Many opportunities can be similar to others but because there is only one you, there is never any effort that is identical. Please know that when God has a blessing with your name on it, it won't pass you up. It is yours in the right time. Keep the faith and continue to do the work.

Today's Affirmation:
WHAT IS FOR ME IS MINE!

Day 173

"Changed behavior is the only indication of an authentic apology."

Actions speak louder than words. If someone gives you an apology but doesn't put in the effort to change their behavior that apology is worthless. That means it is time to reconsider this relationship. Also keep in mind if you're the one in the place that feels the need to apologize make sure your intentions are in a space to actually change your behavior. Otherwise it's a waste of air and energy.

Today's Affirmation:
I SHOW UP AS MY AUTHENTIC SELF!

Day 174

"There is an art in knowing when to fall back and focus on you."

The best way for this to be discovered is through communication. Make sure it is not based on assumptions. However, it is also important to make sure that the action in their behavior correlates with their words. If not, it may be time to put the energy back into yourself. You can't lose when you invest in you.

Today's Affirmation:
I AM MY NUMBER ONE FAN!

Day 175

"Expressions of gratitude is a quick way of attracting better into your reality."

The universe/God will continue to rush abundance in our present when the energy of gratitude is expressed for the things your currently have. Because there isn't a spirit of lack. Look at the glass as half full. You already have everything you need. Just look around.

Today's Affirmation:
I AM BLESSED!

Day 176

"Enjoy your life like you don't have enough fingers to count all of your blessings."

Life has its inevitable ups and downs, highs and lows. But what goes down always finds its way back up. Understand that you are blessed. Even if you're in a low right now just know that you will be on your way back up. Only a matter of time. Keep the faith.

Today's Affirmation:

I AM ALWAYS TAKEN CARE OF!

Day 177

"Sometimes you have to break your heart to save your soul."

Everything happens for a reason and the way it is supposed to. We experience situations where we are hurt by other humans or by situations that may not be in our control. But what we can control is the choice to learn from them. Walk away with more knowledge and soul growth to move into the next chapter in life.

Today's Affirmation:
I HAVE FAITH IN ME!

Day 178

"Create the energy you want around you."

If things are looking low for you right now, I encourage you to write a list. Take some time and focus on your situation. What can you change? What is in your control? That's what you should put your energy to. Anything else doesn't deserve your energy or time. If everything is on the up, keep it up and start writing manifestations to add to your blooming abundance.

Today's Affirmation:
I AM ABUNDANT IN ALL AREAS OF THIS LIFE!

Day 179

"One positive thought could affect the outcome of your entire day."

The best way to set the tone for the day is by setting your intention for the day. Before you get up for the day decide what you want your day to be like. Tell yourself it will be one of the best days of your life and have faith and watch it unfold.

Today's Affirmation:
TODAY IS THE FIRST DAY OF THE REST OF MY LIFE!

Day 180

"Having a good day starts with the belief that it can actually happen."

Anything you believe you can create. It all starts with you. Wake up with intentions of having a good day and your day will be great.

Today's Affirmation:
I CREATE MY REALITY!

Day 181

"Telling the truth won't cost anything but dishonesty could cost you everything."

With lying you run the risk of being exposed. You also don't want to be in a place where your integrity is questioned. Because one lie could cost you many things you may value in life. From friendships, to money, to opportunities. When challenged by honesty just keep in mind the risk versus the temporary reward.

Today's Affirmation:
I STAY TRUE TO MYSELF!

Day 182

"Life has no limits, there is nothing you can't be, do, or have."

Trust the process. Focus on the work and not the time. Remain diligent. Have faith and your dreams will be realized.

Today's Affirmation:
I ATTRACT EVERYTHING THAT IS GOOD FOR ME!

Day 183

"Life is a movie, make it good by taking control of the script."

You have the power to shift the things you're not satisfied with. As long as you're alive you can take the smallest steps to implement change. Let go of the fear and start making it happen.

Today's Affirmation:
I AM COURAGEOUS!

Day 184

"Don't waste your time leading horses to water if they don't trust themselves enough to know when it's time to drink."

I t's hard to come to terms that we all don't vibrate on the same frequency. Life is ever progressing but some people get left behind in the process when they just aren't on the same wavelength. That is okay. Sometimes they catch up and other times they don't. Just keep pushing forward and maybe they will catch up.

Today's Affirmation:
I AM BETTER EVERY DAY!

Day 185

"A person can only love you at the level in which they love themselves."

This is why it is important to first love yourself. That way you are able to meet your own needs first and second communicate to others how they can meet them too. Self-love is the best love.

Today's Affirmation:
I AM ALWAYS CHOSEN!

Day 186

"A second chance is like an expensive gift, everybody isn't worth the money or the time, choose wisely who you're just giving them out to."

Some situations are lessons for us to learn that aid in our growth it doesn't necessarily mean we are supposed to revisit those situations or force them to work. Take the time to evaluate a second chance given. Second chances come with an increased risk. Choose wisely.

Today's Affirmation:
I AM THE BEST VERSION OF MYSELF TODAY!

Day 187

"If thoughts create your reality, do you like what you see? If not, what are you telling yourself?"

Research states the average person has about 60,000 thoughts per day. These thoughts really become a reflection of how we feel about ourselves and what we tell ourselves. Make sure what you're telling yourself is just as loving as the things you tell the people around you.

Today's Affirmation:
I LOVE MYSELF AS I LOVE THOSE AROUND ME AND SOMETIMES MORE!

Day 188

"You are your own competition, utilize your time to create an elevated version of yourself."

There is nothing you cannot do that you have put a thought too. If you believe you can achieve. Do not kill your dreams before you have put in the effort to try. Also, at the first sign of hardship do not quit. You owe it to yourself. Don't give up on yourself.

Today's Affirmation:
I OWE IT TO MYSELF TO ACHIEVE GREAT THINGS!

Day 189

"Significant transformations require experiences, be grateful for the good and the bad because they make you who you are."

Through the progression many of us go into situations where we are protective and want to avoid the bad. This is almost impossible because it is the wave of life. Things will be on the up and things will be on the down. Just know that you are built to endure all of it.

Today's Affirmation:
I AM BUILT TO WIN!

Day 190

"Tell them to request a refund if they call themselves betting against you."

When people doubt your potential, it is always best to use it as fuel to fire up your path. Let the naysayers do what they do best and continue to prove them wrong.

Today's Affirmation:
I AM POWERFUL!

Day 191

"Don't accept constructive criticism from those who haven't built anything for themselves."

Experience is key when it comes to most things. It is hard to take advice for face value if the person can't relate to the situation. Some well put together packages can also be empty. Take everything with a grain of salt and consult with the person you should trust the most. You.

Today's Affirmation:
I TRUST MYSELF TO MAKE THE RIGHT
DECISION FOR ME!

Day 192

"Never let the fear of dropping the ball keep you from playing the game."

You are here at this very moment because you are supposed to be. Never let your thoughts of fear, doubt or insecurity lead you to believe otherwise. Mistakes are made to perfect the task and to give an opportunity to be skilled in your craft.

Today's Affirmation:
I AM SURROUNDED BY THOSE WHO LOVE AND CARE FOR ME!

Day 193

"It is hard to start a new chapter in your life if you keep going back to read the old one."

Life is about progression. If your thoughts are in a loop about what has already happened it's going to be difficult to do anything different or move forward. Make peace with the past and let it go. You have stuff to do and it doesn't involve you focusing on the old. It's time to move forward with the new.

Today's Affirmation:
MY FLAWS MAKE ME UNIQUE!

Day 194

"Don't put your life on hold waiting for things to change. Create the change while still enjoying your life."

So many people put their life on hold. Saying oh when I lose this amount of weight I am going to do this or when I get this amount of money I am going to do that. Life is short, you can accomplish and set goals while still living. Forget what other people think. You deserve happiness today.

Today's Affirmation:
I AM SECURE IN MY MIND AND SPIRIT!

Day 195

"Stay focused on where you're going and have appreciation for where you have been."

Have faith that the universe/God is leading you down the right path. Do not get distracted by the moments of the past. Understand they were meant to propel you forward and it's hard to move forward if you keep looking back. The prize is ahead and you are one step closer.

Today's Affirmation:
I WILL ACCOMPLISH AL GOALS I SET FORTH!

Day 196

"Some people won't like you because the light they see in you threatens the darkness that resides in them."

J ealousy is a sick disease and sometimes it is difficult to recognize those who are suffering from it. Don't allow it to pollute your energy. When you come across it get rid of it. Whether it is coming from another person or situation, it is never healthy. Continue to be the light.

Today's Affirmation:
TODAY I CHOOSE JOY!

Day 197

"I am always good, even on my worst days."

There is so much power in gratitude. Even you aren't feeling like this quote is true. Say it to yourself until you believe it. There is something around you that will bring you joy even in a time of turmoil. Try to find it and remember tough times don't last.

Today's Affirmation:
I AM GREATER THAN MY BIGGEST TRIBULATION!

Day 198

"Choosing your mate will make or break your future so choose wisely."

Choosing a mate can definitely make or break you. That decision also has a lot to do with how you feel about yourself. If you're in a loving relationship, you may be a witness to your own personal revolution which is a beautiful thing. If you're with the wrong person you may feel stagnant or even like burden. Choose wisely who you want to share your energy with.

Today's Affirmation:
MY SOULMATE IS PERFECT FOR ME!

Day 199

"Stay focused on the goal and trust the process."

Most of the time when we reach a goal the way we get there is not always with a clear path. Many times, it came with a string of events that were not the prettiest. People don't really see the struggle but want to revel in the outcome. Not realizing the blood sweat and tears you put into it. Know that you deserve the outcome and that all of those struggle days and nights made it what it was. Give yourself credit.

Today's Affirmation:
I REAP THE BENEFITS OF MY WORK!

Day 200

"It took what I been through to get to what I'm going through now. through it all I take it and smile."

Having faith in the journey is believing in the promises of God/the universe. Knowing that everything is working in your favor. And that all trials are built to make you better. You got this. Smile because you know what is coming.

Today's Affirmation:
I AM BUILT WITH RESILIENCE!

Day 201

Fill up your tank.

Take some time at the end of your day to write about anything for five minutes straight. Pour on to that piece of paper anything that is in your heart that needs to be let out. Whether it is a love letter or hate letter to an individual. Maybe a love letter to yourself or a family member? Whatever it is get it out. Once it's done, if you know you don't want to return to it, either burn it or flush it. Check in with yourself and see how you feel after that release.

Today's Affirmation:
LET GO AND LET GOD!

Day 202

"Only stay where the love resides."

Without loyalty, trust and respect it is hard to have love. Love is a combination of all of these things. Love is how we should treat people in our daily interactions. If people are determined to hurt or harm you mentally, spiritually and physically it is up to you to remove yourself from those situations. Don't dwell in places that don't serve you.

Today's Affirmation:

I AM WORTHY OF RESPECT, LOYALTY, AND TRUST!

Day 203

"The beauty that is found in the process of our cultivates the joy that is felt in the outcome."

It takes time to finesse your goals into reality. This can be a multiple step process. Keep moving forward in what you can control to cultivate what you want within this life. You are worthy of it and you will have it. Just don't give up.

Today's Affirmation:
I HAVE THE PATIENCE TO SEE MY WORK THROUGH!

Day 204

"Failure is always an option, how else could you perfect your craft?"

Understand that failing at something holds just as much as weight as winning. Because in actuality in both scenarios you learned something. However when it comes to failing you are at an advantage because you know how not to a second time. Find the beauty in trying again and the knowledge that has been developed through the process.

Today's Affirmation:

I HAVE THE POWER TO MAKE GOOD CHOICES!

Day 205

"Don't just follow the trends, set them."

No one person is exactly alike. That also means that not everyone is going to agree with your taste, lifestyle or habits. But that doesn't matter. You know why? Because you do! Do what feels right in your spirit even if everyone won't agree. Stop waiting for the approval of others to validate your dreams. Your dreams are yours for a reason.

Today's Affirmation:
I ACCOMPLISH ALL GOALS
EFFORTLESSLY!

Day 206

Fill up your tank.

Take some time today to do something exclusively for you. It doesn't have to cost you anything and it doesn't have to involve other people. Anything that is relative to self-care. Some examples of this: watching mindless tv, listening to some music, taking a bath, working out, going for a walk, eating your favorite snack, hanging out with someone you care about or even just giving them a call, looking up comedy skits online that may make you laugh. Whatever it is, do it with the purpose of experiencing joy.

Today's Affirmation:
I CHOOSE TO BE HAPPY TODAY AND
TO LIVE A LIFE FILLED WITH JOY!

Day 207

"The more you give, the more the universe will return to you."

If you are out here grinding day in and day out and doing everything because you move with good intentions, Just know they see you! You are loved and cared for and will reap the benefits of harvest for your hard work and take-charge attitude.

Today's Affirmation:
I SHOW UP AS MY AUTHENTIC SELF!

Day 208

"Never allow excuses to be the reason you don't push forward."

There really is no such thing as a good excuse. It is definitely an oxymoron. Something you should not be giving yourself because nine times out of ten you deserve better. Stop accepting them and stop giving them. You owe it to yourself.

Today's Affirmation:
I AM MY OWN HERO!

Day 209

"Life isn't always great, but the way we react to things can determine if it gets better."

L ife is a full-on roller-coaster ride and if you're still breathing you are definitely on it. When things are sent your way to test your morals, do the unexpected and let it ride out. In one hand don't take disrespect but also don't feed into it either. Life goes down but once it's there the only other way to go is up.

Today's Affirmation:
I CARRY A LIGHT OF TRUTH AND INTEGRITY!

Day 210

"If you live a rebellious lifestyle, then you rebel against things because they go against your ideals and the integrity of your character as a person."

When all else fails, stay true to you. That is true to yourself in mind, body and spirit. Love yourself fully even when people closest to you don't agree with your life decisions. Your life is yours to live and it's a short one so make it count.

Today's Affirmation:
I HAVE THE POWER TO CREATE CHANGE!

Day 211

"Build your dreams or someone will hire you to build theirs."

Working for others is not a bad thing. There is no cut or dry way to accomplish a goal. You can still work for others and follow your dreams. Just put in the same effort into yourself as you would someone else's company.

Today's Affirmation:
MY MONEY GROWS EFFORTLESSLY!

Day 212

"Your direction is more important than your speed."

N o one wants to go fast in the wrong direction. Can you imagine how long it would take to get back and most times those situations end in head on collisions. Take your time, you have the time. Use it wisely so that you don't have to completely start over. There is nothing wrong with starting over but it can be very different if you're starting with the tools you picked up along the way.

Today's Affirmation:
I ATTRACT THOSE WHO RESPECT ME!

Day 213

"Forget trying to impress, let the work you cultivate and the words you speak inspire!"

People pleasing can be bad for your health if you start to lose yourself in the process. Sometimes you have to say no to certain situations to stay true to yourself. What others think of you does not override what you think and how you feel about yourself. People will notice when they need to. What's most important is how you feel about yourself.

Today's Affirmation:
I LOVE ME JUST AS I AM!

Day 214

"Life is a balance of holding on and letting go."

The most pertinent thing about this is knowing when to. Don't let your pride get in the way causing you to release things that should be staying and don't let fear allow you to hold on to things that are leaving you stagnant.

Today's Affirmation:
I ONLY HOLD ON TO WHAT IS GOOD
FOR ME!

Day 215

"Don't talk about forever, talk about today."

It's good to have an idea of what you want in the future but don't get stuck there. All we have is now. What can we be doing now? Because when we are stuck in the future we are in worry and when we are stuck in the past we live in regret. So stay in the present where the gift resides.

Today's Affirmation:
I REMAIN IN THE PRESENT!

Day 216

"Real eyes realize real lies."

Intuition is a very real thing. It is our sixth sense that comes from our spiritual self to keep us out of danger. However it can easily be confused with the ego. But when you're getting a feeling that someone is not showing up authentically for you and you're catching contradictory statements and actions you need to maneuver from that situation before it becomes worse. Forgive but don't forget.

Today's Affirmation:
I ONLY ATTRACT TRUTH IN MY LIFE!

Day 217

"Be you and do you for you."

There is no love like self-love. Self-love is the best love because once its cultivated to its high vibration it begins to reflect in your daily life. Do for you, what you want others to do. Show up for you, love on you, care on you. The longest relationship you will have will be with yourself.

Today's affirmation:
I CHOOSE TO LET GO OF ANGER!

Day 218

"Something is always better on the other side of letting go."

The fear of letting go is very real. Mostly because it is almost impossible to see what is on the other side. This is where faith comes in. Trust in your higher power. Whether that is God, the universe or yourself. Just know that a totally new life is on the other side of letting go what no longer serves you as well as things that are not in your control.

Today's Affirmation:
THE BEST IS YET TO COME!

Day 219

"Blessings overflow significantly when you operate with pure intentions."

Do all things with good intentions. Operate from a space of love. Although the reciprocation doesn't happen right away every time please know that the laws of karma are on your side.

Today's Affirmation:
I AM GRATEFUL FOR EVERY SECOND OF MY LIFE!

Day 220

"Carrying childhood trauma into adulthood can lead to childish relationships, release it for your future self."

Have you seen an adult throw a tantrum? Have you been that adult throwing the tantrum? Guilty. Some individuals had pleasant childhoods with secure parents that allowed there inner child to be nurtured in cared for and then there is us. A lot of times when we are acting from a space of turmoil where we can control our emotions it's because of some unresolved issue within. Take time to spend with yourself to figure that out. In the long run it can open up some space and opportunity for you to get to the root of the problem and potentially break generational curses. What do you have to lose?

Today's Affirmation:
TODAY I CHOOSE PEACE!

Day 221

"No matter how your day goes remember tomorrow will always bring a blank page for a fresh start."

Yesterday is gone and because of that you have been blessed with an opportunity to start with a clean slate. It's up to you to take the step forward and cultivating the change you want in your reality. You can do it. You have all the tools and are more than capable. Even if it's just the thought and the idea. That still means something. Show up as who you strive to be today and let go of what you may have been ashamed of from yesterday.

Today's Affirmation:
MY FEELINGS MATTER!

Day 222

"Let go, have faith and let God/the universe take care of it."

There is no worry with faith. You can't pray for something asking God/the universe to help you or manifest a dream and then start worrying. There is no room for that. Have faith in knowing that everything in the world is working for you and not against you. Let it ride out like you know it's yours.

Today's Affirmation:
I BELIEVE AND TRUST IN MYSELF!

Day 223

"Lions don't react when Chihuahuas bark."

Everyone is vibrating on different frequencies. There is definitely levels to this game called life. Don't allow those who have yet to reach your level talk down to you. The only way you hear them is if you turn back. And we are not doing any of that. We are on a mission. If they have something to say they will catch up if it's meant for you to hear it.

Today's Affirmation:
I AM SAFE AND SECURE!

Day 224

*"You were born alone, and you die alone, don't be
uncomfortable with sitting with yourself."*

There is no relationship guaranteed like the one you will have with yourself. You have to be for you first and everyone else comes next. GOD, you, and everybody else. You can't love others efficiently without first having a love for God and for yourself.

Today's Affirmation:
I AM WORTHY OF RESPECT!

Day 225

"Remember if something is making you unhappy change it, whatever you're not changing, you're choosing."

Never settle for holding on to things that don't make you happy. Anyone that is not adding, anyone that is taking away from you, and this goes for mentally, spiritually and physically, tell them to move around.

Today's Affirmation:
TODAY WILL BE A GOOD DAY!

Day 226

"There is always a reason for gratitude, what's yours?"

E ven on your worst days there is something to be grateful for. When you are in a rut just try to find one thing that you are grateful for. Or one thing you will be grateful for. Speak your healing into existence.

Today's Affirmation:
I DESERVE SUCCESS!

Day 227

"Find reasons to stay motivated, small or big, use the reason as a way to stay gassed up."

There has to be something around you that motivates you. Is it a song? Your family? Maybe your friends? You could just be you! That's really all you need. You are worth the reason to stay motivated to stay on the grind for whatever it is you want in life.

Today's Affirmation:
TODAY I AM CONFIDENT!

Day 228

*"Don't stop, get it, get it. Leave the excuses and
always come through with it."*

Excuses are just a way to slow down. If
they are given to you, find a way
around. If you find yourself making
them, find a way around. You can have
whatever you want; stop talking yourself out of
it. There are several ways to accomplish a goal.
If one way isn't working move on to the next.
But you got this!

Today's Affirmation:
I GIVE GRATITUDE FOR MY LIFE!

Day 229

"Never lose yourself in any relationship, stay true to who you are and allow the people around you to love the real you."

The beauty of you as a person is the fact that you are an original. You know how much originals of anything are worth? That is you. So why show up as anything or anyone else? Allow people to see the real you and they can choose to deal with it or not. Whether they stay or leave it is still a blessing.

Today's Affirmation:
I AM GRATEFUL THAT I HAVE THE POWER TO CHANGE WHAT I DON'T LIKE!

Day 230

"Why chase when you can attract? Step into knowing what is for you is for you without a shadow of doubt."

Knowing what you want is one thing believing you will receive it is another. Once you have decided you can have something regardless of the cost or ways to obtain it God/ the universe will conspire so that you receive it. All it takes is the desire and the knowing.

Today's Affirmation:
I ALWAYS DO MY BEST!

Day 231

"Life's riches and wealth come from things that are considered priceless."

What makes people happy differs from person to person. But it's usually the simple things that money can't buy. Laughing with a friend, being able to go for a walk, hugging a loved one. Take the time to do something today that money can't buy.

Today's Affirmation:
I AM SO PROUD OF MYSELF!

Day 232

"Forget what other people think, do what makes you feel at peace."

Everyone is not going to agree with what you decide is best for you. It's hard for them to completely understand the decisions you make. You want to know why? Because you are you and they are them. Do what makes you happy and stop letting others opinions have control over that.

Today's Affirmation:
I AM THE CREATOR OF THE LIFE I WANT!

Day 233

"When all else fails remember you are still breathing so you still have time to win."

Every day is a new day. If yesterday, last month or last year are done and gone. You have time to start your day one if you want to. You are alive there is still time for you to be doing whatever it is that you want to do. The key is knowing you can and not being consumed with doubts. You got this.

Today's Affirmation:
I HAVE THE POWER TO OVERCOME ANY CHALLENGES!

Day 234

"Know that everything you put out into the universe returns double so do everything with loving intentions."

Karma can be good or bad. It's all based on your intention. So, decide which karma you want to receive.

Today's Affirmation:
TODAY WILL BE BETTER THAN
YESTERDAY!

Day 235

"The love you seek in others never forget to give more of that to yourself first."

Love you first so that you can properly love others. You can't pour out of an empty cup. And if no one has ever told you, you are worthy of love and peace and happiness.

Today's Affirmation:
I AM VALUABLE!

Day 236

"People come in our lives for lessons and blessings, and they are often only around for a season, and I guarantee it's always for a specific reason."

Some of us have friendships that ended after twenty years and best friends you have only known for a year. Everything happens for a reason and relationships and human interaction is not exempt from this. It may hurt letting go of certain situations but in due time you will understand why it didn't work or they may end up coming back. Just turn the focus on you and look forward to all the good people you have in your life today.

Today's Affirmation:
I HAVE ENDLESS OPPORTUNITIES!

Day 237

"You are who you believe you are capable of being."

In order to realize your dreams, you have to visualize yourself in that place. If you can't see yourself in that place, how would you ever get there? Focus on believing you can have the things you want. That is how they will become a reality.

Today's Affirmation:
I AM B EAUTIFUL INSIDE AND OUT!

Day 238

"Our value is only limited by who we perceive ourselves to be, stop thinking clearance thoughts and giving people discounts."

You are worth more than any monetary value. It's time to start moving like it so others can fall in line.

Today's Affirmation:
I FIND PROSPERITY IN EVERYTHING I DO!

Day 239

"Your past is done and gone, this will never dictate who you are and what you're worth today."

The good thing about yesterday is that it will never happen again. Especially in the case that it didn't go well. You get another day, another opportunity to do something different. Take advantage and don't worry about what happen yesterday. You are smarter today because of it.

Today's Affirmation:
I HAVE THE STRENGTH TO MOVE FORWARD IN LIFE!

Day 240

"Regardless of what you have done and what anyone has said never forget you are priceless. Period!"

There isn't any amount of money that anyone could come up with that will still measure your worth. You are one of a kind. Authentic and there is no one out here like you. Start moving like you know that.

Today's Affirmation:
I CREATE MY OWN POSITIVE ENERGY!

Day 241

"You have to move different when you want different."

Change what you can and release what you can't. If you don't like the way things are going, change it. If you can change it right away plan for the change. Either way, you are in control. You are in the driver's seat. You got this.

Today's Affirmation:
I AM IN CONTROL OF MY LIFE!

Day 242

"Your mind has to arrive at your destination before your life does."

Mindset is everything. You want to be healthy; you have to think healthy. You want to be rich; you have to think rich. Place your mind in that space to be ready to receive whatever it is you want. Its already yours, what are you waiting for?

Today's Affirmation:
I REMAIN PRESENT IN THE MOMENT AND DON'T WORRY ABOUT THE FUTURE!

Day 243

"Be selective in your battles for sometimes peace is better than being right."

Some people are committed to never seeing things from your perspective. And you know what, that is okay. However there is a difference between constructive criticism from people who have your best interest and those who are just looking for an argument. Don't waste your energy. Somethings just don't need to be explained and are not worth your time.

Today's Affirmation:
I AM SURROUNDED BY GOOD PEOPLE!

Day 244

"Nobody watches you harder than the people who can't stand you."

Keep giving them something to watch. There is a thin line between love and hate. They really admire you and can't help themselves. Pray for them.

Today's Affirmation:
I AM BECOMING THE PERSON I DESIRE TO BE!

Day 245

"You're always one decision away from having a totally different life."

Be the change you want to see for yourself. Start by really digging deep and discovering what you want for yourself. You can have it. Know that and believe that. If things aren't going well, you have that power to make it different.

Today's Affirmation:
MY HEART IS OPEN TO LOVE!

Day 246

"Be confident in your ability to manifest."

Things can find a way to flourish completely in private. Keeping them to yourself may not be a bad thing. Use the time to learn how to trust yourself to watch your greatest desires start from ideas into fruition.

Today's Affirmation:
I SHOW MY BODY LOVE AND
RESPECT!

Day 247

"You can have a friend for seventeen days and a friend for seventeen years. Friendships that are built to last reflect high in quality."

It is a very special to have a long-lasting friendship or relationship. Because they tend to be rare. Cherish those you have been able to grow and glow with.

Today's Affirmation:
I HAVE INNER STRENGTH AND SERENITY!

Day 248

"Real love gives you butterflies, not heartache."

Love comes from God. God is love. Love does not hurt. Don't allow anyone to hurt you and tell you it's love. That's not what God intended it to be.

Today's Affirmation:
GOD HAS MY BACK!

Day 249

"Your attitude can make or break your attractiveness."

Beauty comes from within. If you move with ill intent and harbor ill will towards others and yourself this will radiate in your spirit no matter how attractive your shell is. Be beautiful because of who you are not by the way you look.

Today's Affirmation:
KARMA WORKS IN MY FAVOR ALWAYS!

Day 250

"If you are still breathing, you have time to level up."

You are here for a reason. Don't settle for the minimum. You aren't minimum. You are worth more than gold. Act like it. Level up!

Today's Affirmation:
I AM A WINNER IN EVERY SITUATION!

Day 251

"You're never asking for too much in life. Believe and know that you are worthy whether others see it or not."

When you get the first no, don't quit until you receive a yes. Those who love you will support you when they see your effort. Don't Give up and surround yourself with winners who want you to win.

Today's Affirmation:
I AM ABUNDANT IN EVERY SEASON!

Day 252

"Sometimes deciding who you are is deciding who you will never be again."

L ife is about progression. Physically you have no choice but to grow. But mentally the elevation is up to you. Every day is a new opportunity to do and be something different. Take advantage.

Today's Affirmation:
MY FINANCES CONTINUE TO GROW EVERY DAY!

Day 253

"You can be the total package that was just mishandled by the carrier."

When things go wrong make sure you look at the bigger picture. It's not always your fault. Sometimes situations and circumstances happen because we are surrounded by the wrong people or are in the wrong places. Just adjust and set an intention and you will find yourself back on the path intended for you.

Today's Affirmation:
I AM SURROUNDED BY PEACE AND CALMNESS!

Day 254

"If you want to go fast, go alone, if you want to go far go together."

There will always be people along your journey divinely placed in your path to help you along the way. If you know they have good intentions and are here for your growth allow them to assist on your behalf. None of us our beneath support. Your most successful mentor received help. Your most famous idol received help. Allowing others to support is a sign of strength.

Today's Affirmation:
I ALLOW MYSELF TO FEEL JOY!

Day 255

"Goals will always be realized if you get up and pursue them."

The first part of going after your dreams is making up your mind to take the first step. Whatever that looks like for you. Make sure that step includes faith and passion and the belief that you can do this. What are you waiting for?

Today's affirmation:
EVERY STEP I TAKE IS IMPROVING
MY LIFE!

Day 256

"The key to getting ahead in life is simply to get started."

There is a lot of fear that goes into failure. But there is nothing to fear. Failure just means you have the experience and you're a little more knowledgeable in the area. So ultimately you are ahead of the game. Take that leap and don't fear falling because you can always get back up.

Today's Affirmation:
I AM AMAZING!

Day 257

"Haters cannot be heard if you are too far ahead."

People aren't always going to like you, nor are they always going to agree with you. Which is fine. Let them be. Focus on the things and the people that are important to you. Let the haters waste their time and remember always give them something to look at and talk about.

Today's Affirmation:
EVERY PERSON THAT ENTERS MY LIFE IS FOR MY HIGHEST GOOD!

Day 258

"Life is forever changing, growing through those changes is an option, what will you choose?"

There will always be adjustments. Some we will see coming and some we won't. The thing that matters most is how we respond in those moments. Remember it is okay to not always be 100%. It's okay to fluctuate between happy and sad. That is a part of life. Just don't give up on yourself. Keep striving and living through life's fluctuations.

Today's Affirmation:
I LOVE AND APPRECIATE MY BODY!

Day 259

"The only thing more powerful than the will to win is the faith to begin."

Trust yourself. The way you put trust in other people and regular things. Trust that you have the power to start and finish anything you want and desire. The first part is knowing and trusting in yourself. You got this!

Today's Affirmation:
I AM MOTIVATED!

Day 260

"If you're going to do things that count you don't have the time to stop and count them. Keep grinding."

Always give yourself a pat on the back and celebrate small wins but keep pushing towards the ultimate goal.

Today's Affirmation:
I AM CONFIDENT!

Day 261

"The person who lacks the courage to start is already finished."

You won't know if you will ever reach your goals if you don't try. What do you have to lose? You will gain experience even if the full dream isn't realized. So in turn you will still win in the end.

Today's Affirmation:
NOTHING IS STOPPING ME FROM
MEETING MY GOALS!

Day 262

"Don't just fall in love with anyone, fall in love with the one who will catch you."

Relationships are an important part of life. However falling in love can be a very scary situation especially if it hasn't worked in your favor. Choose wisely and know exactly what you want when it comes to your needs. Make sure the person can meet those needs or has a desire to do so. No one wants to be in a one-sided situation. Use your intuition and take your time.

Today's Affirmation:
I AM SUCCESSFUL IN ALL AREAS OF MY LIFE!

Day 263

"No man or woman is worth your tears and the one who is wouldn't make you cry."

Healthy relationships are pivotal to your wellbeing. If an interaction with an individual is making you more sad than happy it may not be worth it. Take some time out to evaluate the situation and make a decision if it's worth being in.

Today's Affirmation:
LIFE IS MY GREATEST TEACHER!

Day 264

*"If someone is wasting your time remember it's the
only debt that cannot be repaid."*

We have life lessons and encounter situations to learn from them. Don't allow repeated experiences with people to keep presenting themselves. It's not worth your time or energy. Granted with energy there are ways to replenish it however with time, not so much.

Today's Affirmation:
I AM BETTER EVERY SECOND!

Day 265

"Allow the difficult parts of life to make you better not bitter."

Forgiveness is always for you, never the other person. Remember resentment is like drinking poison and waiting for the other person to die. Don't let situations with people or circumstances make you a resentful person. Remember all aspects of life are for our growth. Even the bad ones. Embrace them because they help you.

Today's Affirmation:
I AM ALWAYS GOING IN THE RIGHT DIRECTION!

Day 266

"Sometimes we need those tough days to appreciate the good ones."

Although life is about good and bad days, and we may or may not understand this process it doesn't mean we aren't allowed to feel in those bad times. Human emotions are meant to happen. So don't shame yourself for feeling sad, angry or hurt. This is a part of life experiences and you are a human. Give yourself some grace and compassion.

Today's Affirmation:
I LOVE ME UNCONDITIONALLY!

Day 267

"Success only comes when you master failing."

Most individuals have viewed failing as a bad thing. When it turns, it creates a better, more informed you. Ideally we all want things to go right the first time and when they don't we feel defeated. This is because most people in success only brag about their wins and never their losses. Understand that the losses will prep you for your wins. You will get there as long as you don't quit. Keep going. You got this and you will be happy that you did.

Today's Affirmation:
I AM SURROUNDED BY LOVE!

Day 268

"Hatred is like a boomerang which is sure to hit you harder if you keep throwing it."

Being a hater is the most unproductive thing anyone can be. It takes away from focusing on the things you want for yourself as an individual. Hating takes up too much time and creates nothing. Just don't do it. It's a waste and won't change anything in your life or theirs. Let it go and move forward.

Today's Affirmation:
MY HAPPINESS RADIATES FROM
WITHIN!

Day 269

"Time spent getting even could be put towards getting ahead."

Let the universe/God handle the laws of karma. You have better things to work on. Let the situation go and let God handle it.

Today's Affirmation:
I HAVE A LOT TO BE PROUD OF!

Day 270

"Be alert and be of service, what means the most in life is what we can do for others."

Giving can be better than receiving. Be a blessing to someone else and witness the good karma unfold.

Today's Affirmation:

I AM SURROUNDED BY GOOD KARMA!

Day 271

"Brilliant people talk about their ideas. Average people talk about things. Small people talk about other people."

Which one will you choose to be today? Every day you choose who you are and set your intention. Make it a productive choice.

Today's Affirmation:

I AM EMPOWERED BY EVERYTHING I DO IN LIFE!

Day 272

"Bosses have the courage to take action where others simply hesitate."

B oss isn't just a title. It's a way of life. Boss up and move in your purpose. Take action and have the courage to push through anything. Boss is a state of mind. If you believe you are one, well start moving like it.

Today's Affirmation:
THERE IS NO OBSTACLE THAT WILL KEEP ME FROM SUCCEEDING!

Day 273

"A real boss faces the music, even when he doesn't like the tune."

Being a boss won't be an easy feat all the time. Some things will flow when you're in your purpose and other things will become trials you have to learn from. Face them all head on. You have the power to succeed in all areas. Push through even if the path has resistance. You are strong enough to push through it.

Today's Affirmation:
MY CIRCUMSTANCES ALWAYS
IMPROVE!

Day 274

"God gave us two ears and one mouth so that we can hear twice as much as we say."

L isten with intention. It's a healthy way to have a conversation and the quickest way to learn something.

Today's Affirmation:
I AM WONDERFULLY MADE!

Day 275

"Some people sleep to dream of realizing their goals and the Bosses stay awake and body them."

Sleep is a necessary practice for your health and livelihood. But procrastination and stalling can be detrimental to achieving your goals. Don't sleep on your dreams or your goals. Get up, get to planning and get to action. Put that first foot forward and even ask for help if you have to. The time is now. This is your sign. What are you waiting for?

Today's Affirmation:
I RELEASE ANY FEARS OF REJECTION!

Day 276

"Life would be much different if we learned how to love people and use things opposed to using people and loving things."

There is so much value in relationships and they are priceless. Cherish the people you love in your life. Things are temporary and can be taken away at any time. Hold value to the things that feed your heart and soul.

Today's Affirmation:
I MAKE THE BEST DECISIONS FOR MYSELF!

Day 277

"The quickest way to happiness is to live in a state of gratitude."

When we appreciate the things we have, we long for nothing and we are blessed in everything. Being grateful for what you have around you allows you to focus on the glass being half full in life opposed to half empty.

Today's Affirmation:
I MANIFEST EVERYTHING WITH EASE!

Day 278

"Realize you have the courage to take your life to the places that scare you."

Have faith in yourself. Don't allow negative thoughts to create a fear that does not exist. Let the what ifs go and take that leap. Trust that you have everything you need within you to make it happen.

Today's Affirmation:
I HAVE NO NEED TO COMPARE MYSELF TO OTHERS!

Day 279

"Don't stress over the could haves, if it should have then it would have."

Sometimes Gods rejection is in alignment with Gods protection. The things we thing are good for us may have hurt us in the end. So when it feels like we lost something in actuality it was a gain. God saw the future before we could and He saved us.

Today's Affirmation:
I RELEASE OLD HABITS I WANT TO CHANGE!

Day 280

"Don't let the small minds convince you that your dreams are too big."

Sometimes the goals we have set for ourselves intimidate those around us. This is mostly because they can't see it for themselves. Don't let their lack of inspiration dim your light. Keep shining and keep knowing you are on the road to big things.

Today's Affirmation:
I AM SMART!

Day 281

"Always be proud of who you are and don't allow someone to shame you based on how they see you."

Perception can be deceiving. Stay true to who you are. Always show up as you with good intentions and no one can tell you who you are if you are confident in knowing yourself.

Today's Affirmation:
I AM HEALTHY!

Day 282

"Don't pay for any subscriptions to other people's personal issues."

It's good to be a supportive friend but not at the expense of your own sanity. Be supportive but don't take on their baggage. You have your own stuff to unpack.

Today's Affirmation:
I AM A MONEY MAGNET!

Day 283

"Get away from toxic people who speak on how you reacted when they are quiet on what they did to trigger you."

Anger is a true emotion that makes us human. This is not something we are supposed to suppress or pretend it doesn't exist. This is also a protective emotion. So don't allow people who antagonize you to make you feel bad for feeling this emotion. Ideally we want to protect our energy and not allow it to transfer. But that is not always the case. Protect yourself, your energy and your space at all costs.

Today's Affirmation:
I AM MY NUMBER ONE FAN!

Day 284

"Remember life gives us what we can handle, so if you are going through a lot, it means you're the shit!"

God/the universe will only allow us to bear what he knows we can handle. All of this is a part of a greater plan for soul growth and progress. Whatever you feel like is wearing you down in the moment look at it as preparation for something greater. You got this!

Today's Affirmation:
MY ENERGY IS LIMITLESS!

Day 285

"Don't worry about your glass being half full or half empty just remember that you are the one who is capable of refilling it."

We have the power to change how we view any situation. Especially if changing the situation is out of our control. We can view it from a different lens. Looking at the glass as half full shows that you aren't completely empty and still have something to keep pushing for. You are valued and loved. Remember that!

Today's Affirmation:
I AM A FORCE!

Day 286

"The only thing that matters is that you believe in yourself."

First and foremost. Everything else comes second. Have confidence in you. Have confidence in who you are and what you possess. Know that you are the ish and you were made for something greater. Keep knowing that and watch everything fall in place. But you have to believe it. You have to know it.

Today's Affirmation:
I HOLD INFINITE POWER!

Day 287

"Failure is success loading."

There can be no success without learning from your failures. It provides us with the knowledge of what works and what doesn't work. We have to change the way we look at failure. In reality failures are blessings that are preparing you for something greater.

Today's Affirmation:
I BELIEVE IN ME WHOLEHEARTIDLY!

Day 288

"Dreams will never work unless you do."

Faith without works is dead. Not literally dead. It just never grows. Faith is just a component of believing the work we put in will grow as we are actively making it happen. Make it happen!

Today's Affirmation:
I AM A MAGNET FOR PRODUCTIVE IDEAS!

Day 289

*"Understand that you are a limited edition, act
accordingly!"*

T he beauty that resides in you is the fact that there is no one like you. You are unique so act like it, know it and believe it.

Today's Affirmation:
*I BELIEVE IN MYSELF AND MY
CAPABILITIES!*

Day 290

"If things go wrong, you always will have the tools to make them right."

I t is okay to be emotional when things don't go the way we expect them to. It's a disappointment in an expectation, not necessarily a disappoint in self. You have the time to make things right. Give yourself some grace and get back to it.

Today's Affirmation:
I CELEBRATE ALL WINS, BIG AND SMALL!

Day 291

"Everybody wants to be a diamond but very few want to go through the process of being cut."

Diamonds are very beautiful and expensive, but they go through a process before getting to that point. Greatness is always the result of hard work, dedication and commitment. Don't give up, you are well on your way. Also understand that your greatness is designed by your own perception and what you believe that looks like.

Today's Affirmation:
I AM FEARLESS AND BRAVE!

Day 292

"Don't allow people to try to destroy your character with lies because theirs has been destroyed by the truth."

You have the right to choose who you want to be. No one else has the power to define who you are but you. Live in your truth and don't let other opinions define you.

Today's Affirmation:
I HONOR MY COMMITMENTS TO
MYSELF!

Day 293

"Always go where you are celebrated and never where you are just tolerated."

The world has over seven billion people in it. Tell the people who are treating you like you aren't worthy to move around. Don't give them your time and energy if you know they don't deserve it.

Today's Affirmation:
I AM FEARLESS!

Day 294

"Don't let those who haven't started laugh at you for starting over."

Like attracts like. Stay in a place of focusing on your dreams and don't get distracted by those who haven't even started pursuing theirs. Stay close to those who want to see you win and push you to get there.

Today's Affirmation:
I KEEP AN OPEN MIND AND POSITIVE OUTLOOK!

Day 295

"Make every sacrifice in life except for the ones that cause you to sacrifice who you are."

Stay true to you through all situations. Choose yourself first with everything you do. Some people may not agree or like it but in the end the only person it affects will be you. Remember you are the driver on this road, you have control over your direction and your life. Make the best choice for you and stay true to that.

Today's Affirmation:
EVERYTHING WILL GET DONE JUST
AS I ENVISION IT!

Day 296

"Create opportunities don't waste time hoping and waiting for them."

All of your ideas are good ideas. But that's all they are until you start putting in the work. Push yourself out of that comfort zone and know that you have the power today to make your dreams a reality. Big or small. Your dreams are important and you will see them through. Don't let fear hold you up.

Today's Affirmation:
I AM FEARLESS!

Day 297

"Don't allow verbal apologies to be an excuse for lack of changed behavior."

Actions speak louder than words. Authentic apologies are a reflection of changed behavior. Forgive them but really think if the change is authentic. Because only you have the power to keep allowing it. What will you choose to do?

Today's Affirmation:
I AM AN HONEST AND TRUSTWORTHY PERSON AND SO ARE THE PEOPLE WHO COME INTO MY LIFE!

Day 298

"Everything you're searching for can already be found within you."

Things and people can be temporary. What is permanent is the relationship you have with yourself. Understanding that *you* are wonderfully made in God's image which means we are equipped to accomplish the unthinkable. Know this. Live this. Breathe this and watch your life shift.

Today's Affirmation:
I AM LIMITLESS!

Day 299

"Stop looking at other people's grass and take care of your own if you want it to be greener."

Take care of you first. In order to be a support for other people you have to make sure *you* are good. Take some time out for you. Treat yourself, love yourself and nurture yourself.

Today's Affirmation:
I HAVE TIME TO DO THE THINGS I LOVE!

Day 300

"Every successful milestone and celebration began with the decision to try."

So just based on that, what is stopping you? You are still breathing, you're alive and awake. You have the power to make anything happen at any moment. This is a sign that this this is your moment. Take that jump and have faith you will fly.

Today's Affirmation:
I AM INVINCIBLE!

Day 301

"The way you love yourself will be a reflection of how you want others to love you."

Love yourself and don't settle for half reciprocation. Do not allow people to give you half love because it is a reflection of what they think of themselves. You deserve the best. But give the best to yourself first. Nobody is going to love you the way you love you but they for sure better put in the effort to come close if they want to be in your space.

Today's Affirmation:
I STAY TRUE TO MYSELF IN
EVERYTHING I DO!

Day 302

"The only competition you have is you. Compete with yourself not others."

There is room for everybody to do whatever they want in this lifetime. No one person can stop you from achieving what you want. There is always a solution to the problem and it's up to you to go after it and find it. Understand that you are only in competition with you. So don't get in your own way with self-limiting thoughts and behaviors.

Today's Affirmation:
I AM UNSTOPPABLE!

Day 303

*"Don't allow anyone to tell you who you are, especially
if they have yet to discover themselves."*

There will be some people in the life who are experts on things they have never done or accomplished. They will try to talk you out of your dreams and goals because they did not have the courage to step out and achieve theirs. Don't allow them to sway you off your path.

Today's Affirmation:
I TRUST MYSELF!

Day 304

"Life makes you happy, but it must first consistently make you strong and resilient."

L ife will give you lemons along the way but eventually those sour moments create sweet lemonade. Understand that even the rough parts of life are there to make you progress in life. To make you better if you choose to learn from them and not allow them to make you a victim. Appreciate all life's moments and know they are working for you and not against you.

Today's Affirmation:
LIFE IS ON MY SIDE!

Day 305

"A bird doesn't fear falling out of tree because the trust is in its wings not in the branches."

Self-validation is one of the pivotal points of self-love. When you're able to validate yourself, you trust in the decisions you make knowing they are for your best good.

Today's Affirmation:
I VALIDATE MYSELF!

Day 306

"The wrong one will find you in peace and leave you in pieces, but the right one will find you in pieces and help you reclaim your peace."

Relationships are an important part of life. When we let people in we are so fragile and vulnerable we give people the opportunity to make us or break us. Some of these people become lessons and others become blessings. Sometimes choosing them is out of our control. We can however choose who stays and who leaves. Keep the blessings around and appreciate them while they are here. Allow the lessons to leave and take back your energy.

Today's Affirmation:
I AM SURROUNDED BY LOVING AND AUTHENTIC PEOPLE!

Day 307

"The only way to win with a toxic person is to not play."

Narcissist is a term that has become popular. It has been the pivotal point of conversations about toxic engagements and interactions. The best thing you can do with a toxic person is agree with them and get them out of your space. The best revenge is leveling up.

Today's Affirmation:
MY GOOD DAYS OUTWEIGH MY BAD DAYS!

Day 308

"It's much easier for life to get better through change than by chance."

You have the power to control your life. You don't have to be dictated by your emotions. The only way for this to be your reality is if you make a conscious effort to do something about it. You have time, change it.

Today's Affirmation:
I AM IN CONTROL!

Day 309

"Understand that bad choices come from being human not being a bad person. Don't allow one mistake to have you thinking your journey is over."

Mistakes are a part of life's purpose. They help you grow and create a wisdom to make you a better person. You weren't designed to come into this life to be perfect based on others' standards. You are allowed to make mistakes. It doesn't take away from your value. It actually adds to it. Don't let anyone tell you differently.

Today's Affirmation:
I AM MADE IN GOD'S IMAGE!

Day 310

"Focus and have faith on what could go right instead of creating fear of what hasn't gone wrong."

I t's good to be prepared for the worst but don't ruminate on it so much that it creates your future. Keep your eyes on the prize. Visualize what you want to come to past and know that it's for you and you are worthy of it.

Today's Affirmation:
I AM WORTHY OF ALL TH GOOD
COMING MY WAY!

Day 311

"You are worthy to speak your truth whether people like it or not."

Your truth defines your character and who you are. Not everyone will agree, but the sooner you get into a place of not caring the better. Live by your own life experience and others but stay true to it. Set boundaries around those who try to make you sway from your true self.

Today's Affirmation:
I AM TRUE TO MYSELF BECAUSE I LOVE MYSELF!

Day 312

"Beautiful people aren't always good, but good people are always beautiful."

Beauty is in the eye of the beholder. But when the inside is ugly the shell will soon be exposed. Moving with good intentions is the foundation of being a beautiful person. Beauty is a symptom of your heart and your character not what you look like in the mirror.

Today's Affirmation:
MY BEAUTY STARTS INTERNALLY!

Day 313

"Never chase, always attract. Be the vibes you want in your life, and they will always appear."

What is for you will come to you. There is no life force that can change that. If God has blocked something you thought was for you stand in gratitude now because you were being protected and God has something bigger and better. Have faith and let God show out because you deserve the best

Today's Affirmation:
GOD DOESN'T PLAY WHEN IT COMES TO ME!

Day 314

"Your family and friends don't need a perfect you, they need a happy you. Which one will you choose to be today?"

When you're truly residing in happiness it becomes contagious. Perfection is about pleasing others. Happiness is about pleasing yourself. What is most important to you?

Today's Affirmation:
I CHOOSE HAPPINESS OVER EVERYTHING!

Day 315

"Never choose revenge by trying to destroy another person's peace. Put that energy in finding yours."

Karma will always come full circle. It's a balancing act that is inevitable. You don't have to lift a finger. Seeking revenge puts the energy back into that person. You win when you take your energy back. They don't deserve for you to even have a thought about them let alone a whole plot, let it go. Watch it play out. Trust the process and have faith. You will always win in the end. Especially if you're right within.

Today's Affirmation:
KARMA MAKES ITS OWN MOVES!

Day 316

"Don't disrespect the ancestors who came before you by doubting your own potential. Keep pushing!"

Generational blood lines are a real thing. Most of us come from hard working individuals who sacrificed for their families to create a legacy. Add to that legacy and keep it going. Stand proud in who you are on a daily basis. God choose you to keep it going. What are you waiting for?

Today's Affirmation:
I AM MY ANCESTORS' WILDEST DREAMS!

Day 317

"Your value will always be found in your character and your intention. Not what you look like and definitely not what you have."

People can sense when you move with integrity. It is something that will follow you for the duration of this lifetime. Don't move with Ill motives because people will see right through it. It may seem like a quick fix but long term it can destroy some valuable relationships. Integrity and character can make or break you. Do things with love and boundaries, you won't lose.

Today's Affirmation:
I AM LOVED; THEREFORE, I GIVE LOVE!

Day 318

"Don't waste your time returning energy or matching it, simply walk away and conserve whatever is left."

D on't allow people to drain you. They usually are attempting so this because they have no way of filling themselves so they attempt to take from you. Don't give them that privilege. Love them from a distance and love yourself more.

Today's Affirmation:
I LOVE MYSELF FIRST!

Day 319

*"Change that worrying spirit to a warrior spirit and
kill it."*

Worrying doesn't add a single second
to our lives. But faith will give you
inspiration for a better future.
Neither cost you anything but one will waste a
lot of time. Which one will you choose to have?

Today's Affirmation:
I STAND FIRM ON MY FAITH
PRINCIPLES!

Day 320

"Be proud of yourself for surviving the days that people said you couldn't."

Whenever someone doubts your potential, it's usually based on their own insecurity. But it is also a gift. Hear me out. It gives you an opportunity to prove to them what you know about yourself. That you're a beast and nothing is impossible for you. So, show them!

Today's Affirmation:
I DO THIS WITH NO EFFORT!

Day 321

"Control your mind/ thoughts and you will have control over your life."

You are I control of your life. You can change it at any moment. If you don't like it, do something about it. Come up with a *why* and allow it to fuel you. You deserve the life you want to live. As a spiritual being you deserve it so start thinking like and moving like it.

Today's Affirmation:
I AM WORTHY OF EVERYTHING I WANT!

Day 322

*"The best things in life aren't things money can buy,
most of them come without a price tag."*

Time, love, happiness, peace and joy are a few things money can't buy. Appreciate them and watch them appreciate. These are the things we were placed on this earth for. Give and receive them in abundance.

Today's Affirmation:
I GIVE AND RECEIVE JOY FREELY!

Day 323

"Stop taking baby steps when you know it's time to jump."

Take that risk. You will be rewarded either way, with a lesson of how to do it better or the outcome you were hoping for. You have nothing to lose but time.

Today's Affirmation:
I CHOOSE FAITH OVER FEAR!

Day 324

"Your mind is your greatest weapon; always keep it locked and loaded."

Knowledge is one of the few things that can't be taken away from you. Learn and understand as much as you can. Exercise your mind just as much as your body. It is your greatest weapon and your greatest tool.

Today's Affirmation:
I AM A MAGNET FOR KNOWLEDGE AND WISDOM!

Day 325

"If you have no control over changing a situation then change the way you view it. Remember you are in the driver seat. Take control over what you can."

E very situation has a lesson in it. It always happens for a reason, learn what the universe was trying to teach you.

Today's Affirmation:
I CULTIVATE KNOWLEDGE AND WISDOM!

Day 326

*"When God removes people from your life stop helping
them find their way back in."*

When you learn a lesson leave it don't
repeat it. These situations were left
for a reason. Sometimes these
situations will be ten times worse the second
time just to make sure you don't pick it up
again.

Today's Affirmation:
I DON'T REPEAR LIFE'S LESSONS, I LEARN FROM THEM!

Day 327

"Experience the magic in connecting to yourself and others instead of over analyzing the dots."

I'm guilty of being overly critical of myself or even over analyzing situations. This can be counterproductive at times. It also puts us in a place of missing out on the present moment. Which realistically that's all we have. Enjoy your time with yourself and others. Life is short and we should be living it fully.

Today's Affirmation:
I AM GRATEFUL FOR LIFE!

Day 328

"Remember luxury brands don't have commercials because the people who can afford them aren't sitting around watching tv."

Marketing appeals to a certain audience. Understand that if you aspire to treat yourself and have more. Move like those who have the things you want. Surround yourself with like-minded individuals who will elevate you in your purpose. Let go of those who hold you down and keep you stagnant.

Today's Affirmation:
I AM ELEVATED TO THE NEXT LEVEL WITH EVERY MOVE I MAKE!

Day 329

"Remember you have the power to create a life you look forward to waking up to."

Life is about action and emotion meeting. Negative thoughts can make both of those create a negative life. Move in accordance with the things you want. What does that look like for you? What does a peaceful like look like? Maybe an abundant life? Maybe a happy life? Start writing this things out and start living like you already have them. This is manifestation in motion.

Today's Affirmation:
I HAVE THE LIFE I WANT TO LIVE!

Day 330

"Never be a prisoner of your past it was just a life lesson not a life sentence."

Your past doesn't dictate you. The past is where it is at for a reason. Forgive yourself today. Even if the people around you don't. Understand that everyone makes mistakes and no one is perfect. But every day we get up we have a chance to do something different.

Today's Affirmation:
I AM A BETTER VERSION OF MYSELF EVERYDAY!

Day 331

"Stop making yourself available for places, people and situations that make you feel like shit."

Feed your energy only where it is returned. Stop letting these vampires take from you. Stand your ground and let them know you can't be used. You deserve to have people around you who want to give as much as they take.

Today's Affirmation:

ALL OF MY RELATIONSHPS ARE GIVE AND TAKE!

Day 332

*"Getting what you deserve starts with the belief that
you are worthy enough to receive it."*

No matter what anyone has told you, no matter what you may have done in the past, you're worthy of all your goals, dreams, and desires. Other opinions don't dictate that only you do. You deserve it all and don't allow anyone to have you thinking anything differently.

Today's Affirmation:
*I LIVE A FULL LIFE KNOWING I AM
WORTHY!*

Day 333

"An obstacle is something you see when you take your eyes off the goals you are trying to reach."

Looking back should only be done once you have reached the finish line. Understand what happens in the past does not define who you currently are. You're not even the same person anymore. Stay focused on the prize and reflect once you have met the goal.

Today's Affirmation:
I AM BETTER THAN I WAS
YESTERDAY!

Day 334

"Dream of the person you hope to be but always have appreciation for who you currently are."

It's always a good thing to visualize the better version of yourself but it's hard to do if you don't have appreciation for who you are today and who you were in the past. All of those experiences shaped who you are. Be grateful for that. Understand that you are one of a kind. Flaws and all. Perfectly made in God's image.

Today's Affirmation:
I AM PERFECT BECAUSE OF MY IMPERFECTIONS!

Day 335

"The only way to see a rainbow is to get through the rain."

Rain is going to come and I'm not going to pretend it will be easy because at times it won't. But it will be doable. Remember you won't endure more than you can bear and a trial wouldn't be meant for you if your weren't built to endure it. Know that, live that and breathe that.

Today's Affirmation:
I AM BUILT FOR THIS!

Day 336

"A smart person knows what to say, a wise person knows whether to say it or not."

Some things are better left unsaid. That's why we have two ears and one mouth. Choose your battles wisely. Don't allow situations or conversations to drain you of your energy or to knock you off your path. Stay wise enough to know when certain things and situations are not worthy of your time.

Today's Affirmation:
I SPEND MY TIME WISELY!

Day 337

"Individuals play the game, but strong teams win championships."

Appreciate those who have been placed in your life, good or bad to help you achieve your goals. Everything happens for a reason and the way it is supposed to. It's very rare that someone makes it through this life alone. Teamwork does make the dream work so when in need don't be too prideful to request a helping hand from those who want to see you win.

Today's affirmation:
I AM SURROUNDED BY WINNERS;
MYSELF INCLUDED!

Day 338

"A mouse trap will always provide free cheese."

Use your intuition in all of your decisions. Life is about love and light but the darkness is there to protect you, so don't ignore gut feelings and even things that may be too good to be true. Trust yourself and your ability to protect yourself.

Today's Affirmation:
I TRUST MYSELF!

Day 339

"If you start soon enough you won't have to run to catch up."

Start today. Whatever it is you want in life start it. Even if it's the bare minimum. Rome wasn't built in a day. Take baby steps. You just have to get up.

Today's Affirmation:
ANY STEP IS BETTER THAN NO STEP!

Day 340

"If you keep your head and heart going in the right direction you will never have to worry about your feet."

Every dream, goal or life's changes starts with an intention which comes from the thought which is manifested through the feeling that illuminates in the heart. Get your heart and your mind right and you will see how things fall into place with little to no effort

Today's Affirmation:
GOD IS KNOCKING DOWN DOORS FOR ME!

Day 341

"Most times we aren't responsible for the things that happen to us, but we are responsible for the way we act when they do."

Acting on emotion will deplete your energy especially if it's a negative one. Don't allow those type of encounters to take you out of a space of peace. Remember peace and happiness is always the goal but they will be tested. The only thing we have control over is how we react. Remember that.

Today's Affirmation:
TODAY I CHOOSE PEACE!

Day 342

"Long after school is over, if you're breathing the education will still continue."

School isn't the only place you learn things in life. It only scratches the surface. Most of life's lessons come through experiences. Whether they are our own or those closest to us. Use your life to soak up all the game and wisdom to constantly level up.

Today's Affirmation:
I LEVEL UP DAILY!

Day 343

"Your persistence is your measure of faith within yourself."

Keep going and don't quit. Even if you feel like it's not the way you want it to be. Don't give up. Keep pushing and watch everything you wanted to unfold. It can take a month it can take years but the time will pass any way. Don't give up you will get there.

Today's Affirmation:
THE DAILY GRIND WILL ALWAYS MAKE ME SMILE!

Day 344

"There is not one rule in success that will work if you don't."

S uccess is relative to perspective. That can look like many different things in life. Success can be anything from the amount of money you have, to the amount of free time you have. Whatever that looks like to you build it the way you see fit. Put in the work to create it in your reality. Setup a plan and start today. This is your sign, what are you waiting for?

Today's Affirmation:
THE FRUITS OF MY LABOR ARE
REAPING!

Day 345

"Once you have learned to love yourself you will have learned to live."

Thee is only one you. The relationship you have with you is the only relationship that is guaranteed. So who better to love on you than you? Give yourself the love you deserve and look at the love from others as an added bonus.

Today's Affirmation:
I AM NOT AFRAID OF LOVE!

Day 346

"Kindness and love should be continuous actions and not treated like faucets."

They are the most valuable free things you could give or receive. Give it to yourself first and let it pour out on those around you. However set boundaries for those who may take advantage of it. Remember setting boundaries is an act of love as well.

Today's Affirmation:
I LOVE THROUGH ACTION AND EMOTION!

Day 347

"Faith does not reject failure it just finds a way around it."

Failure is going to happen if it's supposed to. It builds character, it elevates you to a higher level and it's just something that is a part of the process. It brings you closer to your goal and sets the path for those who will come after you. It's a blessing disguise. Let it fuel you.

Today's Affirmation:
MY FAILURES HELP ME LEVEL UP!

Day 348

"Failure is going to happen, but it doesn't have to stop you."

Failures are an inevitable part of success. It is a part of the learning curve. They teach us so much in life. At times it may or may not hurt but understand this part is just as much of a gift as the wins. It builds a stronger smarter you.

Today's Affirmation:
I AM SMARTER EVERYDAY!

Day 349

"Authenticity will always be greater than achievement."

Being yourself is the best thing you could ever become. Being your authentic true self has to be mastered and maintained before you can reach achievement. Staying true to yourself is the true level of success.

Today's Affirmation:
I AM ENOUGH JUST BEING ME!

Day 350

"To be a star you end up giving your best performance in the darkness."

L ow and sad times are going to happen in life. These experiences can be difficult and sometimes life changing. However, we are always strong enough to withstand them. You have the light and power to get through them. Don't give up.

Today's Affirmation:
TODAY I AM STRONG!

Day 351

"Don't worry yourself about tomorrow when today is all you have."

A lot of the time we get into a space of feeling like we have to accomplish certain things before we can start living. All we have is today and you're doing all that you can today. It is enough, you are enough. Tomorrow will come, all we have is right now and today. Take a moment to enjoy it.

Today's Affirmation:
I AM CALM, EVEN IN DIFFICULT SITUATIONS!

Day 352

"Don't worry if you feel like you're headed in the wrong direction remember God/ the universe is okay with U-turns."

E very day is a new day. As long as we wake up the next day, we have an opportunity to change it. You don't have to condemn yourself for things you may have done that weren't perfect. You have the opportunity to change your ideals and yourself. Be loving to yourself and understand that we all make mistakes. It's all a learning process.

Today's Affirmation:
TODAY I AM CHOOSING HAPPINESS!

Day 353

"Minds are like parachutes they only can be filled with opportunities when they are open."

Be open to learning from any experience that crosses your path. Understand that things do not happen by accident. Receive the signs that are gifted to us by the universe. Whether this comes from a person or just an experience, understand it is teaching you something.

Today's Affirmation:
EVERYDAY I AM MORE CONFIDENT
IN MYSELF!

Day 354

"Life is like farming so it is important to understand you can't reap what you sow in a single day."

There is so much work that goes into reaping a harvest. It also takes time and patience. Little by little, day by day. A lot of the time we want immediate results, but some things take time and cultivation in order to have the best outcome. Be patient and understand you took the first step to lead you on the right path. The goal is ahead but don't rush it and enjoy the process.

Today's Affirmation:
I AM GRATEFUL FOR DREAMS THAT HAVE TURNED INTO REALITY!

Day 355

"If you want to feel rich, just count all of the things you have that money can't buy."

Gratitude is important in life. There are so many things that we have right in front of us that are priceless. Whether that is the love for self, love with friends, Moments of laughter, a hug or a dance. These are things that fill our soul up with pure joy. Take the time to appreciate the little things that mean so much.

Today's Affirmation:
I AM SURROUNDED BY LOVE!

Day 356

"Stop saying someday like it is a day of the week."

All we have is today, there are twenty-four hours within it. Now what are you going to do with it? Tomorrow is not guaranteed, and yesterday is gone. Take that step in moving forward. Don't live with the "what ifs" when you have the time to start today. What are you waiting for?

Today's Affirmation:
I AM ACCOMPLISHING MY GOALS!

Day 357

"Consistent worry will get you to one place ahead of your time, an early trip to the cemetery."

Worry about the things that are in your control. If they aren't in your control you don't need to be worried. Worrying does not increase time nor does it pay the bills. Being attentive and cautious are healthy actions worrying is not.

Today's Affirmation:
I AM DIVINELY GUIDED IN ALL THAT I DO!

Day 358

"A winner makes a commitment while losers are making promises."

Mean what you say and say what you mean. Make your words turn into live action so that you're not eating them later. Stay committed to your goals and aspirations and most importantly stay committed to yourself by standing by your words.

Today's Affirmation:
WINNING IS EASY FOR ME!

Day 359

"The man sitting on top of the world got there by first standing up."

D on't give up. The difference between you and the person who realized their dreams is that they didn't quit. Your time will be your time but don't stop working towards it. Don't stop putting in the groundwork. You are worthy of it. Remember that and know that!

Today's Affirmation:
I AM AN EXPRESSION OF SUCCESS!

Day 360

"You get in life what you have the courage to ask for."

There is a 50/50 chance that you will get the answer you have been wanting. So just ask. What do you have to lose? The answer can be no, the answer can be yes, or it can be not right now. But you won't know unless you ask. What are you waiting for?

Today's Affirmation:
EVERY DAY I CREATE MY OWN PATH, I AM IN CONTROL!

Day 361

"Growth is when you realize a new year isn't going to change you until you are ready to change yourself."

Take a leap and step out on faith. If you want something different it's up to you to make it happen stop waiting for something to move if you haven't gotten up. Even if it is the smallest change just take that chance and do it. You are experiencing this life now. What are you waiting for?

Today's Affirmation:
TODAY I WILL CRUSH A GOAL!

Day 362

"Start off being humble and being kind but always check anybody who gets out of line."

The saying *treat people how you want to be treated* rings true in the beginning. However, if someone is not respecting you in the process then that saying goes right out the door with them. Set boundaries and set the ground rules for the way you should be treated so that no one forgets.

Today's Affirmation:
I AM WORTHY OF RESPECT!

Day 363

*"Remember those who chop you up behind your back
are behind you for a reason. Keep it pushing."*

People have very little to say about people who aren't doing anything in life. Keep living, loving and grinding. In other words, keep the haters entertained and keep giving them something to talk about.

Today's Affirmation:
*I AM WORTHY OF ALL LIFE'S
BLESSINGS!*

Day 364

"Let the universe/God fight your battles; Karma doesn't need an address."

Sometimes the best thing to do in a situation that has soured is to just let it go and let God. There isn't much that could be said to a person who is committed to being right opposed to understanding. You may never get that apology. So, are you going to stop living because of that? No, keep it moving.

Today's Affirmation:
EVERYDAY I CHOOSE HAPPINESS!

Day 365

For the last fill your tank:

Write out some affirmations that you enjoyed in the book and place them where you can see them daily. If you're on the path of manifesting money write some about money, If you want peace put some on sticky notes about peace. Whatever journey you're on, stay on that path by utilizing the affirmations written in the book. This is simply to remind you of the power you already possess.

Today's Affirmation:
I AM THE CRRATOR OF THE LIFE I WANT TO LIVE!

About the Author

Jai Marie Harris has always stepped up to the plate when it came to defeating the odds stacked against her. Knowing to every problem there is a solution. As a single mom who was raised by a single mom statistically her life shouldn't be where it is today. For her she identifies it as being blessed opposed to luck. Being the first in her family to not only obtain her Bachelor of Science and Master of Science degree from Howard University, Jai Marie also always kept faith and inspiration at the forefront of this journey called life. As an Occupational Therapist and business owner, she has elevated to a place of being able to provide the motivation to her patients. But she didn't want to stop there. With a ton of inspiration that she receives from her family and friends Jai Marie knew the words she had been inspired by and passing on to patients had to be put to paper. As the Author of "The Spiritual Gas Up," Jai Marie's prayer with writing this book was that more people would be inspired through daily quotes, affirmations, and daily gas ups. This is in hopes to keep the masses motivated through this lifelong journey of always centering your peace around yourself. Living by her mantra of anything is possible. Jai Marie Just wants to inspire other individuals that no matter the circumstances, where you are in life, anything is also possible for you.